SPECIMEN HUNTER'S HANDBOOK

Late evening, a time when the big ones move. An angler waits patiently for a bite.

SPECIMEN HUNTER'S HANDBOOK
A SPECIALIST ANGLERS GUIDE TO BIG FISH

Edited by Trevor Housby

BLANDFORD
LONDON · NEW YORK · SYDNEY

First published in the UK 1987 by Blandford Press
an imprint of Cassell plc,
Artillery House, Artillery Row, London SW1P 1RT.

First published in paperback 1988.

Copyright © 1987 Blandford Press

Distributed in the United States by
Sterling Publishing Co, Inc,
2 Park Avenue, New York, NY 10016

Distributed in Australia by
Capricorn Link (Australia) Pty Ltd
PO Box 665, Lane Cove, NSW 2066

British Library Cataloguing in Publication Data

Specimen Hunter's handbook : an anglers guide to big fish
I. Housby, Trevor
799.1 2   SH684

ISBN 0 7137 2094 8

All rights reserved.
No part of this book may be reproduced
or transmitted in any form or by any means,
electronic or mechanical, including photocopying,
recording or any information storage and
retrieval system, without permission in
writing from the Publisher.

Typeset by Kevin O'Connor

Printed in Great Britain by
Anchor Brendon Ltd, Tiptree, Essex

CONTENTS

1 · BARBEL   Andy Orme   7

2 · BREAM   Graham Marsden   20

3 · CARP   Chris Yates   36

4 · CHUB   Arthur Clarke   48

5 · EEL   Trevor Housby   67

6 · PERCH   Trevor Housby   79

7 · PIKE   Mike Booth   95

8 · ROACH   John Wilson   117

9 · TENCH   Bob Church   133

INDEX   141

1
BARBEL
by Andy Orme

I caught my first barbel when I was twelve years old, and although it weighed less than 2lb the memory of the bite, tremendous fight and sheer wonder at its beauty is still vivid. That little Kennet fish certainly started something, because for the next twenty years I fished for barbel wherever and whenever I could. This mania has taken me to some fine rivers: Dorset Stour, Hampshire Avon, Thames, Kennet, Severn and many other lovely but less well-known haunts of 'Old Whiskers'.

Today the barbel is the quarry of a growing band of enthusiasts, a fact reflected in the existence of two specialist clubs, the Barbel Catchers and the Association of Barbel Enthusiasts. Such anglers are attracted by their streamlined powerful looks, their stunning fighting ability and the sheer challenge of trying to catch them.

LOCATION – NATIONAL

The distribution of barbel in Britain today has been influenced by two main factors: the last ice age and human activity. It was about 20,000 years ago when ice last covered most of Britain. When the weather became warmer and the ice receded, east England was connected to Europe by land and the Thames, for example, was a tributary of the River Rhine. As the ice disappeared, fish recolonised Britain by swimming up the rivers. Five thousand years ago the sea level had risen to such an extent that Britain became an island.

Now you can see why it is our eastern rivers like the Trent, the

Thames and those in Yorkshire contain barbel, while many of the southern and western rivers do not. Those that do, and the Dorset Stour, Hampshire Avon and Severn are included, owe their barbel populations to direct introductions by man.

Although barbel seem to be able to live and grow in still water they cannot breed, and so the majority of populations are still in rivers.

LOCATION – LOCAL

Within any river, some stretches hold a lot more barbel than others. Very slow reaches with a muddy bottom contain very few. Fast areas with plenty of gravel and streamer weed often support huge shoals of small to average size fish, but in my experience the biggest fish occupy river sections where the flow is moderate but enough to maintain a clean gravel bed. These sections are often relatively deep, but are also quite heavily weeded.

It is vital to appreciate that the location of barbel varies throughout the year and also throughout a 24-hour period. I split my barbel season up into summer, autumn and winter fishing, which involves June to August, September to November, and December to March respectively.

In the summer months many barbel are found in the fast, heavily-weeded areas, but as the weed dies back in autumn and the rain increases river flow they tend to move to more sedate, deeper stretches. During the winter their location can vary enormously due to flood conditions, but I shall describe that later.

Barbel like shelter. During daylight, in natural conditions, for every barbel exposed on a gravel run there will be half a dozen hidden in the weed or holed up under the bank. Under cover of darkness they feel secure and will move out into areas where you may never see them while the sun is up. This behaviour should influence your choice of swim and also your choice of how to fish, especially with regard to baits.

BAITS FOR BARBEL

There are three main types of baits used for barbel: 'specials', 'naturals' and 'particles'. Whichever is selected should reflect the river conditions which influence the natural feeding behaviour of the barbel.

I believe that there is a natural feeding pattern over a 24-hour period. During daylight barbel rarely feed, but may have occasional feeding spells. At dusk they begin feeding in earnest, and this continues through the night, sometimes until dawn.

What this means to the barbel fisherman is that during the daytime he must make the fish feed, and there is no doubt that particle baits are the type most likely to do it. Why they work I do not know, but I suspect that the presence of hundreds of tiny food items may imitate natural phenomena like a hatch of insects. Whatever the reason, it works. Non-feeding shoals of barbel that are hiding under weed can be lured out onto gravel runs and made to feed by introducing quantities of particles.

Maggots, casters, sweetcorn, hemp and tares are the most common of these baits, but diced luncheon meat, chopped worms and

A deep winter double barbel on the ground.

HNV (high nutritive value) baits in particle size have been successful. Combinations of different baits can be deadly, and feeding hemp and corn on the hook particularly so.

I reserve the use of 'naturals' and 'specials' to conditions or times when I suspect that the barbel will be feeding anyway. Sometimes that is during the day, especially when the rivers are high and coloured following heavy rain, but normally it is at night.

Lobworms are the most commonly used natural baits, and rightly so; they are a superb bait but excel when hundreds have been introduced as feed. This was the technique exploited by the old Thames anglers of yesteryear. Other naturals include slugs, crayfish, lamprey larvae, loach and minnows. All have been known to catch barbel but they are a neglected group of baits, probably because it takes quite a lot of effort to collect them.

Under the category of 'specials' I include luncheon meat and chopped ham with pork. They are tough baits, relatively heavy, easily obtained and cut into shape, and are highly successful. Care must be taken when selecting brands, though, because some float! Tesco's 'chopped ham with pork' is very effective, but you must make sure that lumps of gristle don't obscure the hook point. Danish blue cheese paste is another deadly bait in the right conditions, and so can be some of the HNV baits. If you make some, ensure that you use heavy ingredients, because you obviously don't want your baits to float off downstream.

A word of caution about new baits in barbel fishing. It seems that barbel, unlike carp, do not indulge in much 'curiosity feeding' and they may ignore a new bait for a long time. I have known anglers to feed a stretch with HNV baits and never get the barbel onto them. Clearly much more needs to be known before firm recommendations can be made. If you can only make a few trips to a water I would advise you to use a bait that the barbel will immediately recognise as food.

Whatever the bait, groundbaiting can be vital. I have already said that particles can stimulate barbel to feed, but if they are already feeding you still need to introduce feed to get them onto your hook bait. Accuracy is vital because you want to attract the fish into your swim and encourage them to search for more food. This can be difficult in fast rivers, but 'bait delivery systems', such as block end feeders for maggots (see Fig. 1) or PVA stringers for specials, can be used to good effect.

It is impossible to suggest how much feed to introduce because it

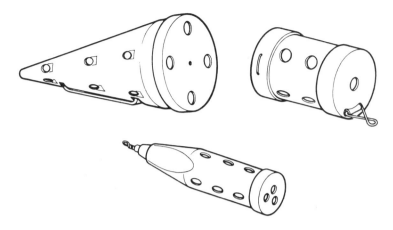

Fig. 1 A selection of block end feeders.

varies from river to river and from season to season. On the River Severn or the Royal Fishery, two or even three gallons of maggots may be required, but on other waters the age-old advice of 'little and often' would be best.

TACTICS AND TACKLE
The most exciting way to catch barbel is to get them on the float by trotting baits through fast weedy swims (see Fig. 2). A nice long gravel run surrounded by barbel-holding streamer weed is the type to find. A constant stream of particles such as maggots will entice the barbel out onto the run, where they will take a bait bounced naturally over the gravel.

Choice of tackle is critical. It must be balanced because fine lines and small hooks are needed to present small baits properly, and so your rod must be able to protect the line and hook hold from the powerful fight of the barbel.

Never go below 3lb line or you will lose too many fish. A 12 or 13ft carbon rod capable of picking up line on the strike and with some strength in the middle section for playing barbel is ideal. I carry a range of balsas and Avons from 2 BB to 5 SSG and find that these cope with most situations (see Fig. 3). For fast swims I bulk most of the shot about 18 to 24in from the hook, but place a number 4 about 6in from the bait to give a degree of control.

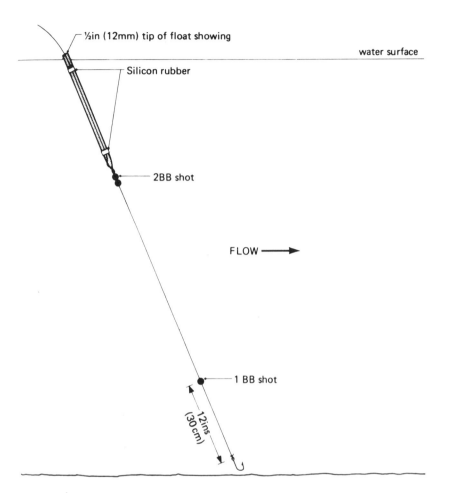

Fig. 2 Float fishing for barbel.

My favourite bait is three succulent maggots on a strong fine wired 14 hook. The float is fished double rubber, over depth and is held back slightly. This results in a bait that trundles over the gravel towards the feeding barbel. Every trot down, I feed the run with a portion of maggots from a dropper or by hand if the swim is shallow enough. Bites are usually very positive; the float dives under and stays there!

Many swims cannot be float fished, or simply respond better to ledgering. If particle fishing a spot for a while, two rods can be used by placing them in parallel on buzzer bars that have been wrapped in tape. 10 or 11ft through-action carbons with a test curve of 1 or

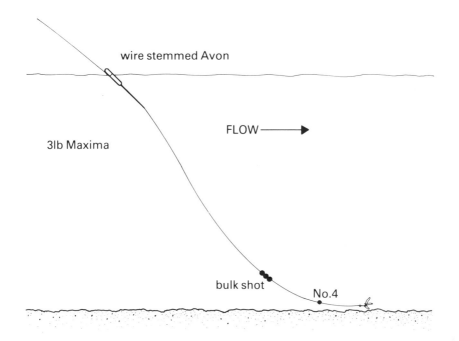

Fig. 3   Simple trotting rig for shallow swim.

1¼lb are suitable, although some anglers prefer longer rods. Placing the rods so that the tips are almost touching means that bites will not be missed. Quiver tips can be used if bites are subtle, and isotopes can be attached to the rod tops for night fishing.

Strong tackle is vital to barbeling (see Fig. 4). Main line for

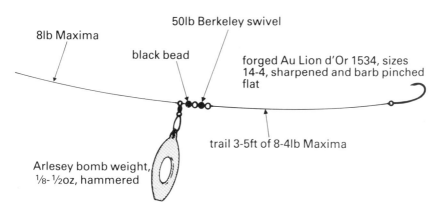

Fig. 4   Ledger rig. All knots are grinners.

ledgering should be 8lb or 6lb and hooks should be forged. Maxima or Sylcast are good lines but the former needs changing regularly because its softness leads to abrasion. Sylcast is tougher but I find it less easy to use because it is not supple. Au Lion d'Or 1534s are still very useful and popular hooks, but other more modern designs like Kamatzus are gaining use.

Tackle should be checked and rechecked during every session to eliminate any weak spots. Stop shots or ledger stops that pinch the line are out. It is far better to use a bead and swivel. Grinner knots are far superior to simple half block knots.

Feeders can often tangle and weaken line. To avoid this a short piece of stiff nylon, say about 12lb BS, can be tied between two swivels below the feeder (see Fig. 5). The stiff line helps to prevent tangles, but should one still occur 12lb line is less likely to break than your trace of, for example, 5lb line.

For ledgering, a range of weights from ⅛ to 1½ oz should cater for all conditions. Pear-shaped or Arlesey bomb-shaped weights are good but are better if hammered to make them flat on two sides. This allows you to control how much they roll about, and they do not seem to catch up on weed much either.

Straightforward ledgering is the technique I use for my favourite method of barbel fishing — roving from swim to swim. This is best when you suspect that the fish are in feeding mood already and don't need to be made to feed by introducing quantities of particles.

A simple ledger rig is versatile and enables almost any swim to be tackled. Too many anglers ignore heavy weed but a ledger rig with

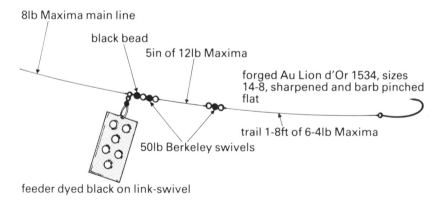

Fig. 5   Feeder rig. All knots are grinners.

Ken Townley and a near double-figure Royalty barbel taken at last light on maggot.

a trail of a few inches can be bombed through weed onto the barbel-holding gravel below. The rod has to be held for this type of fishing because the constant pull of swaying weed can mask bites. If you hold the rod and feel the line, it is possible to identify the pull of a taking fish. You can also feel if the lead is holding on gravel and is not buried in weed.

When roving, explore every swim for a minimum of 10 to 15 minutes and then move on to another. In the right conditions barbel will definitely be feeding; it is up to you to find them. No bites may mean that you are wasting time in the wrong place.

This roving about has produced some wonderful catches for me, including ten Middle Avon fish in a day. Five were caught on consecutive casts and one was a double.

I make a point of always trying a new swim even if it looks lousy. Some have produced eye-opening results, and on a couple of occasions my best fish from a particular stretch has come like this. If in doubt, stick a bait in the water; you just never know what may be lurking beneath those gurgling waters.

MODERN RIGS

Carp fishermen have developed two rigs of special use to barbel fishing. The hair rig has now been used by barbel men for a few years. On some waters it has greatly increased the catch rates, especially when used for particle 'bashing' with hemp and corn. Personally I am shifting my viewpoint on the rig. I have used it successfully for several different types of fish, but to be honest I think it makes fishing too easy.

Chris Yates believes that it is unethical. After all, do we want a challenge or not when we go fishing? Surely part of the pleasure is getting an elusive wild animal to take a bait with a hook on it. Chris, I'm beginning to think that you are right; however, if anyone reading this simply wants to increase their catch rate and doesn't care how they do it, by all means use the 'hair'.

The second rig refined by carp fishermen but used unwittingly by barbel anglers for decades is the bolt rig. In its simplest form a heavy lead is placed very near the bait — just what people used to do when they got the so-called typical barbel bite of the rod nearly being pulled out of the rest as a fish hooked itself.

Bolt rigs with a fixed lead are unsuitable for barbel, because should the lead become stuck in the heavy weed or some other snag the hook link will snap like cotton when the barbel lunges. A free-running lead at least allows you some time to free it, should it become stuck.

PLAYING BARBEL

The strength of barbel is undisputed and it is reflected in their streamlined muscular bodies that are adapted to exploit the strong currents they may live in. Combine these facts with their liking for areas of dense weed and you have problems trying to land them once hooked. The two golden rules are: never apply too much pressure, and always pull downstream.

Barbel are perverse. The harder you pull they harder they pull back, so it is best to maintain light pressure and gently guide them downstream and into a sheltered area of water to be netted. Sometimes they get stuck in weed. When this happens simply maintain light pressure with the rod tip slightly bent and wait until you feel the fish 'kick', then apply more pressure and try to haul the barbel free. It may take several attempts but you will do it in the end.

Correct playing technique is particularly important when float fishing because the tackle is relatively light. It is vital to select the right swim to fish in the first place, because it is pointless hooking a barbel on 3lb line in a weedy swim if you cannot walk below the fish and play it downstream. It is impossible to haul them upstream through weed on light gear.

WINTER FISHING

In winter playing barbel is not too problematical because most of the weed has gone. The major hassles are location and timing. Although barbel will feed occasionally in cold conditions they feed much more regularly during mild spells when the water temperature is 6° C or more.

Luckily for us barbel men, mild winter conditions usually coincide with other conditions that make barbel feed — high, coloured water conditions. Floods in winter often follow warm torrential rain that has been blown in on westerly winds from the Atlantic. Barbel definitely feed well at these times but they also

Andy Orme holding a perfect winter 13lb 7oz barbel.

avoid the main force of the winter currents; slacks, eddies and sheltered areas on the inside of bends are the places to find them.

It is well worth the effort to squelch your way through the flooded fields and hang your gear on bushes or fences, because in winter barbel are deep and heavy. At this time of year you are in with a great chance of a lurker. Some of my best barbel have been taken in the depths of winter. I'll never forget looking down on that glistening January-caught 13-pounder from the Middle Avon.

Winter barbeling is essentially opportunistic; wait for the best conditions and then when they arrive fish your heart out.

HANDLING BARBEL

Although barbel fight like tigers and are perceived as tough strong creatures, they are especially prone to damage by anglers. There are structural and physiological reasons for this. The first ray of the dorsal fin is serrated and easily gets caught up in netting. Fine, soft mesh nets are the only acceptable type, but these take a bit of getting used to in strong conditions. Barbel should never ever be put in keepnets. (Match anglers, please note that.)

Apart from damage to the dorsal fin, many barbel fight themselves to a state of exhaustion. This is because they do not have large enough energy reserves, and those that they do have take a long time to replace. After they have been played, landed, unhooked, weighed, photographed and generally admired they need careful nursing before being released to fend for themselves. Hold them, head facing upstream, for as long as it takes to get them swimming strongly off into the main current.

GOING FOR A 'DOUBLE'

As yet no single tackle exists to sort out bigger barbel from their smaller cousins. If you want specimen barbel it is all down to location. The best rivers in the south are the Hampshire Avon and Dorset Stour but it is only certain stretches that regularly produce the biggest fish. Homework is essential; walk the banks, talk to people and read every book and article on the subject. It is the only way.

2
BREAM
by Graham Marsden

In the last decade or so a number of giant bream, up to the current British best, an incredible 15lb 10oz fish, have come from a handful of waters, all but one in the southern half of the country. The one exception is a Staffordshire mere which has produced bream to 15lb 6oz.

In this same period specimen bream fishing has, like all aspects of big fish specialising, increased in popularity more than any other branch of angling, and there is a school of thought that is suggesting that this almost sudden appearance of really huge bream is a direct result of the increase in specimen bream angling pressure.

That big bream fishing has become more popular than ever is not in question, and that this increase in popularity has some bearing on the number of huge bream caught in recent years is also not in doubt, but I contend that the main reason is that such colossal bream have never before existed in such numbers. Not that the giants exist in large numbers, but that there are enough of them in these handful of waters to make the chance of catching them a little better than the chance of finding the proverbial needle in a haystack.

So before we delve into the technicalities of catching big bream, let us first decide whether we want to become proficient big bream anglers, or just anglers with a few giant bream to our credit. One is not necessarily the same as the other. You don't have to be a good angler to sit on the bank of one of the giant bream waters, fish a standard method, and wait for one of them to take your bait. All you need is an ability to accept inactivity for long periods, and a great deal of spare time. I'm not knocking that, but simply pointing

David Ankers returns a specimen 13¼lb bream.

out that that is not the way to becoming a competent big bream angler: you just do not catch enough fish to learn very much.

Far better to fish a water where the bream average 7–9lb, with the odd double a possibility. These fish will probably be members of a reasonably-sized shoal, and as such, once you have some knowledge and experience, will provide consistent sport, presenting you with all the problems associated with catching big bream and giving you all the fun and interest there is in trying to solve them.

Remember this: those huge bream of 12lb plus do not take more skill and experience to catch than bream of 7lb and more. They only take more time. But if you learn your trade before you tackle the giant bream, then that time could be considerably reduced.

LOCATION

Locating the feeding areas is essential to any kind of fishing, but where big bream are concerned it is imperative. Bream have established feeding routes and you must learn the whereabouts of these before you even think of wetting a line. These feeding routes vary in length and pattern, but are invariably more than 25yd from the margins, except where water more than about 8ft deep is found close in.

The feeding routes are not a visible entity; something you could see if you swam to the bottom. But they are there just the same: imaginary railway lines that the bream follow with the same unswerving loyalty as a train going from one station to another. All fish have favourite areas, and patrol from one natural larder to another, but bream do so at very regular times, in tight shoals, like a regiment of soldiers. They can be so predictable that you can plan just where to fish at a particular time on a water, knowing that the bream will pass through that swim within a few minutes either way of the time you expect.

Bream follow these patrol routes even when they are not inclined to feed. It seems that they have to adhere to the ritual of patrolling the feeding grounds in spite of the fact that they may not have an appetite to appease. This accounts for the fact that bream anglers suffer more false bites, due to bream brushing against ledgered lines, than anglers of any other species. Curiously enough, bream anglers suffer more 'line bites' when catching few fish than they do when they are catching successfully.

I've said that these patrol routes are invisible, so how do we discover where they are? Fortunately, the bream has another endearing habit, which is to roll at the surface, sometimes before, often during, and occasionally following, feeding. So what we have to do is to watch the water's surface carefully at dawn and dusk, which are the most likely times the bream will feed and consequently roll.

We have to be vigilant regularly, for bream don't always roll when they feed, but sooner or later they will and eventually we can conceive the pattern and extent of the patrol route, or routes, and decide exactly in which swim we are going to launch our attack.

I have almost always found that the best swims on a patrol route are found at those points where the route deviates, i.e. where it suddenly veers off at a tangent. What happens is that we see the bream rolling in one direction at several points along a 50yd stretch, when they disappear, and suddenly reappear 15yd or more away, going off at right angles to the original direction. Or they may cease rolling at a point and never reappear until the next feeding spell hours later, when they begin to roll again at the start of the route. These points, which I refer to as the turning and terminal points, are usually best of all, with the terminal point being the real hot-spot.

BAITS AND PREBAITING

There are some anglers who scorn the idea of baiting swims for a period before actually fishing, claiming that it makes little or no difference to how successful we are. This, of course, is nonsense, and is usually the claim of a lazy angler who cannot be bothered to prebait. If he did he would soon realise that the exercise is very valuable indeed.

I can see some logic in the claim, however, if one believes that prebaiting is only to attract fish to a swim. After all, why spend time and money trying to attract bream to a swim we know they visit regularly anyway?

Prebaiting is not just an attracting exercise, though: it is mainly educational, in that it teaches fish, in this case bream, that certain foods are in plentiful supply, good to eat and, most important, safe to eat. If we drive home this lesson regularly, then it is to our great advantage when we do eventually go along and offer them that 'safe' and delicious bait, complete with sharp steel enclosed.

The type of bait we use to prebait with and consequently use as hookbait is governed to a great extent by the type of water and how heavily the water is fished. For instance, on private waters which are little fished, bread and worms are excellent, and will usually outfish anything else. However, on waters which are heavily fished, especially those used for contests, where maggots and casters are used by the gallon, there is no point in using anything else. Once bream are introduced to maggots and casters in quantity they become addicted.

But this is no bad thing, for it is possible to continue catching bream for several hours longer than usual by scaling down your tackle and presenting them with tiny baits, which is something you cannot do when using big baits like bread and worms.

It is a fact, too, that bream are much easier to hook on maggot and caster. They are too fond of sucking worms, and particularly bread, to the edge of their lips, whereas with maggot and caster they tend to crush these between their lips even when they don't actually take them inside their mouths, giving us a chance to hook them in either case.

There is a growing trend to use more exotic baits such as the high nutritive value (HNV) baits of the carp angler. I have yet to be convinced that there is any advantage in these baits for bream, and at this juncture would advise anyone to stick to traditional baits until more is known. There is no point in paying a lot of money for high protein and vitamin materials unless the rewards justify it. Bream so often requires such a lot of free feed to keep them feeding in the swim that the cost would be exorbitant. It is too often the case these days to place too much emphasis on bait anyway, when the solution to most angling problems lies in location or technique, or in some other more fundamental reason.

Anyhow, my first choice of bait on not too heavily-fished waters would be bread flake followed by lobworms. Then, once catches began to deteriorate, I would seriously consider feeding heavily with caster and maggot, especially if I had a few friends fishing the water who would go along with me and also feed heavily with caster and maggot. On heavily-fished and match-fished waters I would use caster and maggot immediately.

Whichever one you choose you should feed them into the swim every day if possible for as long as possible before fishing. Three weeks or more of prebaiting every day would be ideal, but one or two weeks of baiting the swim every other day is better than not doing it at all.

As far as quantity is concerned this will depend on the water and the density of the fish stocks. Not just bream, for all the species present will take advantage of free feed. The ideal situation is to be able to inspect the swim after a few days of baiting by running a scoop across the bottom and checking the contents for signs of bait. If you find none, then increase the amount you are feeding. If you

Graham Marsden with a big bream caught on float.

find more than you think you should, then cease feeding altogether until it disappears, and then begin with a smaller quantity, checking the swim once more after a few days.

If it is impossible for you to inspect the swim then you have to take a chance. But always err on the side of too little rather than too much feed.

TACKLE AND TECHNIQUE – LEDGERING

The standard method of fishing for big bream currently is some kind of swimfeeder rig. In fact the swimfeeder has become the standard method for most species, to such an extent that there are specialist anglers who no longer specialise in a species but specialise in the method. Really, they may not realise it, but they have returned to the old 'chuck-and-chance-it' days and don't really care what they pull out as long as it's big. This is fine as long as you're happy doing something that doesn't stretch your imagination and for as long as you can keep kidding yourself you're the bee's knees when you pop a big one out.

Some anglers have built reputations as great bream or tench anglers (sometimes both) solely on the basis of fishing one water with one method. It seems that the only real problem they had was gaining access to a water capable of producing the headline-grabbing giants.

I rarely use a swimfeeder on stillwaters, not simply because of the reasons I've just mentioned, but because I think I can do a better job feeding the swim with a catapult and using more efficient end tackle, and because I get more fun from catching fish by using skills which are not so necessary when 'feederfishing.

I accept though that the swimfeeder has a place on stillwaters, and do not hesitate to use it when I think it can do a better job than I can with other methods. When I do use it I construct the rig as in Fig. 6.

The main thing when 'feeder fishing is accurate casting, which means dropping it in a circle no more than 3yd or so in diameter. It means regular casting too, which I'm a great believer in anyhow (there is more about this later).

Swimfeeders, depending on the type and size, can weigh up to 2oz or so, which means that a suitable rod and line – capable of casting up to this weight over long distances – must be used.

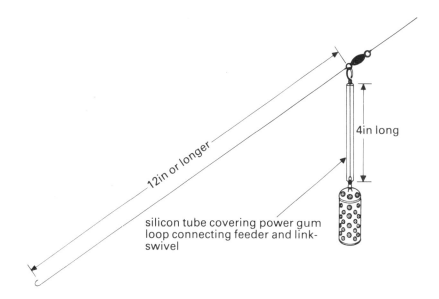

Fig. 6   Swimfeeder rig.

Ideally, the rod will be 11ft long, have a test-curve of about 1¼lb, and will have a fast-taper action. The line from reel to hook length will be a minimum of 5lb, and the hook length somewhat lighter, 3lb to 4lb test being about right according to the presence or otherwise of snags and the fighting ability of the bream, which can vary quite considerably from one water to another. Bream in clear waters seem to fight harder than those in more opaque waters.

My favourite rig is a fixed paternoster tied as in Fig. 7. At one time I favoured the short hook length, long bomb tail style. My taste has changed because I find that I catch a lot of bream while the bait is still falling those last few feet to the bottom, and a long hook length will allow the slow fall of the bait. In fact, it pays to vary the length of the hook length to find out which one encourages the most bites 'on-the-drop', as it is known.

I also like the fixed paternoster because it casts long and accurately, two attributes which are very desirable when bream fishing. This much lighter rig also allows me to use a rod to my liking, i.e. not so stiff, with some feel to it, rather than the almost poker-like action of the fast-taper rod.

Anyway, let me describe an actual breaming session I had quite recently, when I used a fixed paternoster ledger rig. That way you'll

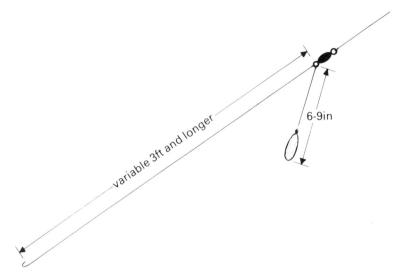

Fig. 7 Fixed paternoster.

learn much about the rest of the tackle and techniques involved.

I arrived for the night session at 7.30pm, in plenty of time before darkness. There was going to be no moon that night, and already a warm south-westerly wind was blowing a good ripple on the surface. It felt close and muggy, the kind of night beloved of bats and gnats; and of me too – it was a night when no respectable bream could refuse to feed.

I chose a swim on the north-easterly bank, the warm wind coming towards me. The swim was an old favourite and had received plenty of prebait, in the shape of brown and white breadcrumb and casters, these past few weeks. A small piece of anchored white polystyrene marked the far edge of the swim, ensuring that the bait was always fed into the same spot.

That night I paddled the boat to the swim and fed in a two-gallon bucketful of brown/white groundbait, and spread two pints of casters over the top.

Back at the bank I tackled up an 11ft, 1lb 2oz test-curve, through-action rod with a 4lb main line and a 3lb hook length. The hook length was 3ft long, and the bomb length 6in, the hook an eyed, size 10, Drennan Blue, which is ideal for flake fishing for bream.

The rod went onto two rod rests, the front one fitted with an optomic bite alarm, following a cast to the 40yd distant swim. Onto

A fine 8lb plus bream for specialist angler Peter Ellery. This fish was caught from Broadlands Lake, Romsey, Hampshire.

a loop of line between bite alarm and reel I clipped on a betalight glow-bobbin. Close at hand, within easy reach of any fold-up chair, I laid down a capacious landing net, bait boxes of maggot and caster, a loaf of sliced white bread, a torch, a weigh-bag and scales, forceps and plastic disgorger, a flask of tea, and a box of sandwiches, and a keep-sack.

I was set for a comfortable and well-organised night session, and as the light faded I was delighted to see the dark humps of one or two bream as they sliced through the surface 30 yds away and headed towards my swim.

It was now 10.30pm, and I knew that I would see and hear my first bite at any moment. All being well it would be a genuine bite and I would catch the first of what could be a good bag of bream on such a promising night. The other possibility was that it would be a 'line' bite, the first of many, and I would struggle to catch bream until the next shoal came through the swim at around 2.30am.

I did miss the first bite, a slow, typically steady bream lift, but recast immediately and latched into a fish 'on-the-drop'! That piece of flake slowly fluttering to the bottom must have looked very attractive. The bream didn't fight exceptionally well, and weighed 7lb 15oz. It was one of the better smaller fish, if that makes any sense, in that it is almost always the shoal of smaller bream, weighing from about 6¾lb to 8lb, that patrol the route first, and at 7lb 15oz it was big for that time of night.

Curiously, although these smaller bream make up the biggest shoals, I rarely seem able to hold them in the swim long enough to catch a hatful. Sure enough, I had one more fish, weighing 7¼lb, a little before midnight, and had to wait for the next shoal to come through at 2.45am before seeing another bite. Then I had a number of line bites as the shoal moved in and settled, before catching just one fish, a nice bream of 8lb 7oz, which was average for that time in the morning in this water, when they usually weigh between 8lb and 9lb. The period I was most looking forward to, however, was 4am when the biggest fish of the lot on this water came through, and, if all went well, could be persuaded by judicious feeding to stay for several hours, depending on the conditions.

They arrived a little early at 3.50am, just when the first faint shimmers of daylight were noticed. The glow-bobbin shot up very fast, not like a bream at all, and the rod rattled in the rests as the fish hooked itself. I was slow off the mark, for I'd been dozing and was slightly disorientated by the bleep of the alarm. I needn't have

A good bream taken from a boat moored close into a bank. This picture shows some of the tackle required!

worried, however, for everything after that went well, and I landed a bream of 9lb 3oz, a lovely fish in peak condition.

The next two hours were extremely frustrating, for there were bream rolling in the swim most of the time and plenty of half-hearted bites that I couldn't hit. It was only when I changed to a 16s hook and double maggots and cast regularly to fish 'on-the-drop' more often, that I hit another bite, a bream of 8lb 2oz. By that time the bream were rolling far less often and bites were tailing off fast. I knew I had to risk delivering them some feed before they lost interest entirely. So out came the Whopper-Dropper catapult, a bucket, and a mix of brown and white crumb liberally dosed with two pints of casters. Small and fluffy balls of this tempting feed were fired into the swim until none remained. Then I waited tensely for something to develop.

Nothing did for several minutes, then I changed from double maggot to caster and maggot on the hook and was rewarded with a good bite I shouldn't have missed, but did. I missed two more good bites and decided to increase my hook length from 3ft to 5ft. The very next cast produced the most positive bite of the morning and I landed a bream of 9lb 1oz.

I had two more bream in the 8lb class before they disappeared, probably for the rest of the day.

TACKLE AND TECHNIQUE – FLOAT FISHING

My favourite rod for float fishing for bream, where there are no snags and it is not necessary to bully the fish, is the Shakespeare 13ft Boron Mach 2 match rod. I like this rod because it allows me to use the fine lines and small hooks that bream demand when feeding in broad daylight.

You see, it is in the full light of day, usually later in the year, September and October, when I do most of my float fishing for bream, usually during those hours when most specimen hunters have packed off home. It is so effective if you do it right you can make some fantastic catches. For instance, in October of 1984 I had three such sessions, two of four hours' duration and one of six hours, all beginning at 10am. In those three sessions I caught 50 bream over 8lb, the biggest at 10lb 2oz.

Swim selection is almost the same, with the exception that you must find a swim close enough to the bank to allow you to float fish

Graham Marsden with a 9lb bream caught on a ledger.

efficiently. I know it is possible to cast 40yd or more with some specially-made floats, but the problem is seeing the float at that distance, particularly when the surface is choppy. So you need to find a swim no more than about 25yd out, or, where possible, use a boat.

Much of my float fishing for bream is done from boats, and the type of swim I look for is a sharp drop-off from shallow to deep water. This allows me to anchor the boat a little way back from the shelf, in the shallow water, but within 15yd of the bottom of the shelf where the bream are likely to feed. The shelf shields me from the fish and also means that hooked fish can be played out in the shallow water away from the rest of the feeding with a 2½lb main line and a 2½lb bottom to begin with, but I'm always prepared to go to 2lb line, or even 1¾lb when the going is really tough. Similarly with hooks I begin with a 16s, but do go to an 18s or even 20s when it is essential. Fortunately, it is a rare to have to drop below an 18s hook to 2lb line.

When the surface is very choppy I prefer the Drennan Drift-beater float, set as in Fig. 8, but otherwise go for the Compolite Hollow-tip, set as in Fig. 9.

The real secret of getting the best out of fairly close-range float fishing for bream is being able to loose-feed. I use casters, and have never yet found a better bait for holding bream in a swim.

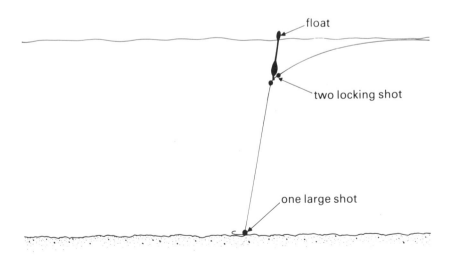

Fig. 8   Driftbeater set-up. Shot size depends on size of float.

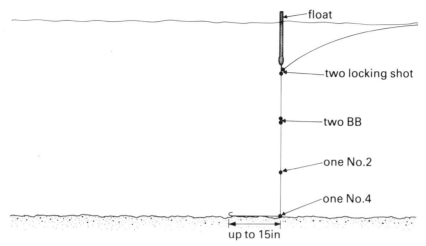

Fig. 9   Hollow-tip set-up.

What I do is lay a light carpet of groundbait, with a pint of casters scattered over the top, and then feed nothing more until I start to catch fish. Then I loose-feed, with a catapult, with almost monotonous regularity, usually every 2 to 3 minutes. I don't fire a lot of casters into the swim each time, unless the bream are feeding ravenously, but I do feed continually. This is very important. I think of it as hypnotic feeding, where you can induce the fish into a mesmeric feeding trance, where they are so preoccupied with feeding they are almost oblivious to their shoal-mates being removed, and tend to throw most of their natural caution to the four winds.

3
CARP

by Chris Yates

Despite instant carp baits, instant carp anglers, instant-hooking rigs, instant carp waters and instant results, carp fishing still retains its original mystique; it remains one of the most exciting and magical branches of our sport. Despite the mind-boggling developments that sometimes threaten to reduce carp fishing to a scientific formula, there is still nothing else that so dramatically mixes the contrast of sustained tranquillity and explosive surprise.

This chapter, then, will not be about 'boileys' (did you enjoy your boiley egg for breakfast?!) or bolt rigs or buzzers or bionic baits or diabolic hair rigs. It will be about uncomplicated carp fishing and about those enduring things that make up the delightful essence of the sport.

Luckily, even on this small island, there is still room enough for every type of fisherman and every style of fishing; it may not be as easy as it was to discover those tranquil, secluded, unpopulated places that can produce good carp as well as give the classic carp fishing atmosphere, but they do still exist. In the south of England, there is a wealth of good fishing to be found in the numerous, quiet ponds that lie dotted throughout the landscape. It seems that the majority of 'serious' carp anglers will always prefer the more familiar, well-flogged big fish waters, and this is fine by me. The more anglers that flock to the monster-haunted pits the more space I'll have to creep round my favourite, willow-shaded farm ponds. Of course I won't catch as many big fish as the pit men, in fact I'll be very fortunate indeed to land anything over 20lb. But I'll net a few double-figure carp, and I'll certainly experience fewer blanks than the pit men. The most important thing, though, is that I will be savouring that vintage quality which makes for classic carp fishing. Just to add extra spice to it all, there is also always the possibility of connecting with something far bigger than you'd expected. After all, Redmire itself was looked upon as nothing more than an overgrown farm pond until the first carp fisher came along and cast his line.

What makes a classic carp water? Well, for a start, it must contain home-grown carp and not be artificially stocked with fish larger than it could naturally sustain. Willow, lilies and reeds are not essential, but they are things that most carp fishers find very attractive on a water. Whatever the bankside vegetation, there should be as much of it as possible; no fisherman should want his carp pool looking like a carefully tended artificial goldfish pond in a trim suburban garden. Naturally, the water should be quiet and peaceful, well off the beaten track, though it is possible to find such places in quite populous areas – park lakes and village ponds, for instance. Ideally, the pool should be of great age; a sense of history obviously accords well with an activity that is more ancient than any other pursuit, except hunting. The perfect pool would, I suppose, be not larger than 5 acres, have extensive shallows, lots of weed (*not* Canadian pond weed), a few deep holes, plenty of large, mature trees around the banks, but with enough open spaces between to allow shrubs, rushes and other bankside vegetation to flourish. Find such a place as this and you will discover the old magic.

As I said earlier, I know of a few such places, but only one of them is exclusive; the rest are club waters, mostly open to anyone who cares to join, and day ticket waters. The first week of the season may find these pools rather more crowded than you would like, but the trick is to wait until the 'busy weather' has blown over; come late July, especially during weekdays, and you'll begin to have the water all to yourself.

Because they are never really hard-fished, these places respond well to most of the standard methods and techniques; ordinary free-lining, ledgering, float-fishing, surface fishing and margin fishing will all bring results. The same is true with baits. There's no need for anything exotic or expensive; all the old favourites will work, some better than others. There's a lovely little pond not far from my home that contains a few biggish and exceedingly cunning carp. These fish get everything imaginable thrown at them, from garden worms to the latest laboratory special, yet I still manage to tempt them on good old floating crust. The secret of it is not really in the bait or tackle, but in location, timing and presentation. I'll demonstrate this in a moment, when I take you fishing with me to a classic water. Of course it's true that bait is important and that some fish would remain almost uncatchable were it not for our increasing knowledge in this area. But too often anglers put all their faith in a special bait and forget about everything else. They lay siege to the fish and just sit back and wait for something to happen. Siege fishing bores me; I prefer to go after my quarry. And when I eventually find him I know, if I've been stealthy enough, that I've got more chance of catching him than if I'd waited for him to make the first move. The carp naturally feels more secure in his own chosen territory than in a baited area where his suspicions would be aroused, however hungry he was, however good the bait.

Stalking up on him unawares, and keeping him in view, I can either drift a floating bait over his head or, if he's feeding on the bottom, drop a slowly sinking bait as near to him as possible and hope that he finds it. If the bait is small and the tackle as light as possible then he won't be disturbed. If the bait is strongly flavoured – but not too strongly – say a bean cooked in paprika or brown bread dabbed with molasses, then the fish will sense it instantly and you won't need to scatter any free offerings about to attract his attention. However, if he's not terribly enthusiastic about food, it often pays off to sprinkle an area a few yards in front of him with a 'mass' bait like maggots or hemp. Two handfuls of maggots followed by a big bunch on a 6 hook has led to the downfall of many a good carp, but I very rarely see any other carp angler using maggots. When I groundbait with hemp I like to use corn or chick-peas on the hook, but I once saw another angler take a tremendous catch of carp, fishing a hemp-caked *cheese ball* over a carpet of hemp.

If the carp is really not interested in feeding then you're wasting your time casting at him. You can usually tell just by looking at him whether he's hungry or not. A hungry carp has his fins erect and looks alert and poised however stationary he is. An uninterested carp will have his fins relaxed, except for his slowly working pectorals; he will look positively droopy. This is why I said timing was important, for so often a carp's feeding times are limited to an hour or two a day, especially during hot, settled weather. If you've timed it wrong it doesn't matter how closely and carefully you've dropped your bait to the carp, he won't bite. In normal summer conditions your best chances are at dawn and evening, though there is often an opportunity of taking a carp in the heat of midday, when the fish

A good hard-fighting specimen carp being brought to the net on the river bank.

are basking in the weeds or lilies. A surface bait deliberately overcast and then inched painstakingly slowly back will often tempt him. Work the bait back until you are too bored to wait longer, but sometimes you will suddenly notice the carp wake to the fact that something tasty is next to it. It often sucks the bait down with no hesitation at all. Usually it then disappears and you strike as the line tightens; sometimes it does not move at all and then you must strike anyway.

The best conditions of all are after a heavy shower has laid the dust of a week's hot weather. Within moments of the rain stopping, the whole pond comes alive and the carp begin avidly feeding. The same sort of thing can occur when a really steady, strong wind blows away a three or four day spell of sultry, still weather. Fish in the margins at the downwind end of the pool, sprinkle in plenty of groundbait, and you could enjoy a magnificent catch. Carp are not disturbed so easily when there's a big wind on the water, and you can often take fish after fish once you've got them concentrated over your baits.

You will appreciate that on a big, deep gravel pit many of the things I've been describing rarely occurs. Only on small, overgrown pools and lakes will you have so many opportunities for spotting and stalking individual fish; only on these kinds of waters will you find that special atmosphere which summons up an instinctive sense that can make the capture of a carp seem almost inevitable, like magic.

But enough of all this dry preamble. Let's go fishing.

This is the place, a perfect pool in every respect. About 3 acres, plenty of bankside cover, including a few magnificent, venerable oak trees; profuse marginal weed and reed growth; sheltered, willow hung channels with shallow, food-rich water; a fair depth off the overgrown dam; extensive beds of soft weeds over the main part of the pond; a nice area of snags where an old boat-house used to stand – you can see all the waterlogged piles poking up through the surface, an ideal safe haven for the carp.

It's a hot, sunny afternoon, not exactly the best time or conditions for productive fishing. But there's enough breeze to ripple the downwind end of the pool and that might be creating just enough extra oxygen in the water to give the carp an appetite.

Beautifully-conditioned common carp.

I've got my rod already tackled up; it's always an advantage, as long as you know roughly what you're going to be doing, to set up your rod and net before you get to the water – so many times I've had an opportunity for a fish almost as soon as I've arrived on the bank and I would have missed a chance, perhaps the only chance of the day, if I then had to fumble about with knots and things. Of course this only usually happens on those lucky days when I catch the carp unawares because there's nobody else on the water. My tackle today couldn't be simpler: an easy-actioned cane rod, a fixed-spool reel loaded with 8lb line and a size 6 hook (eyed) tied with a palomar knot. I've got a light 32in frame net and all my extra tackle and bait is in my jacket pockets.

Even with polarising glasses I don't see anything cruising around under the ripples or basking along these marginal weed and reed beds. We'll creep right under the pool and see what's happening on the far side, and as we go we'll scatter a few handfuls of bait into all the most promising-looking places. Bait? Perhaps the cheapest bait you can buy, mixed pigeon feed – a combination of millet, maples, field beans and corn. A 14lb bag from a pet shop will last me a busy season. I've got about ¼lb in this bait box; it's been cooked in a pressure cooker for fifteen minutes and I added a dessertspoonful of paprika, to add to the flavour. Perhaps it's because it's a variety bait, which the carp aren't accustomed to, that it works so effectively. I've been using it for years and it's worked on every water I've baited with it. My best carp on it was a 27lb common. One special thing to remember if you think of trying it: only use the field beans on the hook, two or three nicked through the skin on a size 8 or 6 (the field beans are the ones with the brown, shiny skin and the dark eye). Obviously the fish are hoovering up all the various offerings in the mix, but for some reason the field beans are the best hook bait, or at least this is my experience. When we sneak back this way, maybe in an hour's time, we may discover one or two fish grubbing about in one of the baited swims.

We have circuited almost the entire pool and we've spotted just one sign of fishy presence, a slight commotion on the edge of this reed bed, merely enough to make the odd stem sway and shake unnaturally. The water is quite shallow here, no more than 2ft deep, so I think it might be worth trying a surface bait. I know the carp is obviously grubbing about around the reed roots, but it often happens that the best way to catch a 'reed rocker' is with a surface and not a bottom bait. I'd like to be truly traditional and use floating crust, but the truth is that, although you still get the odd fish on crust if you persist, most of them are too wary of it to even look at it nowadays. My fault entirely! I've taught dozens of them that bread crust is not good for their peace of mind. Again, it's my local pet shop who supplies me with my needs: Purina *Sea Nip* biscuits (shaped like little fish!) (Rod Hutchinson put me onto

Specialist angler Ron Barnett nets a 'low double' carp from a beautiful but weedy lake.

these) or Chum *Mixer*. Both are deadly baits. Soak them for two or three minutes before you leave home and they're normally soft enough to use by the time you reach the water. I'm using the *Mixer* today. I'll chuck in half a dozen well away from the fish and let the breeze drift them down to him. One, two, three baits float past that little whirling vortex of water. Now the disturbance has stopped and a fourth bait drifts virtually over the top of where the carp should be. Shlomp! Down it goes. Shlomp, shlomp! Down go the other two. Not a long or a difficult cast this one. Any fool could catch this fish, but I'm not giving you the rod. I know it's selfish, but this will, or should be, the first one of the season for me here. They outwitted me last week. Two *Mixers* on the hook, a sideways flick to avoid the overhanging branch and the bait lands in just about the right place. I really need to overcast a little because as the bait drifts downwind the line tends to check it and draw it in slightly. It's all right, though, he's seen or smelt it and he's going straight for it.

Flumsh! What's this? The little rascal. He's not playing the game. Yes, I know, it looked at first as if he'd taken it, but he was just turning abruptly at the last moment and the downswirl sank the bait for a few seconds. I'll have to be a bit more cunning. I said any fool could catch this fish, but maybe this fool is going to be made to look even bigger than you think.

I'll toss in a few more free offerings and this time quickly get the bait in amongst them. Here he comes again, looking serious about it. And look! There were obviously more fish in this reedbed than I guessed. Three, no, *four* more. *Slosh, shlurmp, shluk!* So close, yet still they understand the threat to their leathery lips.

Of course it's fairly obvious, even to me, what the problem is here. The carp are only refusing my bait because there are *two* biscuits on the hook. I'll just sacrifice casting weight and hope I can flick out a single *Mixer* far enough. If I had the time or the patience, perhaps I'd weight the line with a bit of holly twig or something more fiddly. Out go a couple more free biscuits, *plonk* goes the bait, just about far enough. Off they drift, all destined to be processed into carp.

Amazing! They virtually all went under together. The line slides smoothly across the surface and – Wheeee! The moment to get his head away from his sanctuary is straight away, before he really cottons on to what's happened. And now he's heading in the right direction, into open water, I can allow him to blow his top. Twenty yards and the pressure's increased firmly with the finger on the clutch. No, I never back-wind with fixed-spool reel, at least not with this one. Not only does it have a superb clutch, but you'd bust the handle off if wound backwards! (A feature of this exquisite pre-

Reeling in a big carp.

war Altex is not just its fixed spool but it's fixed anti-reverse. I don't mind. I find back-winding not only clumsy but also inefficient. To be perfectly honest, I'd rather not use a fixed-spool reel at all. Centre pins are much more pleasing to handle.)

Enough of this technojaw. The fish is cutting round in a wide arc and unless I can get a good sidestrain on him he'll torpedo me into the reeds for certain. By running to the left as far as I can and winding like a spinning-wheel, the angle of pressure is just enough to roll over and draw him round in front of us. There he goes, you can see he's fully scaled and that he probably weighs around 9 or 10lb. Look at the way he leans away from the pressure and keeps his flank broadside to me; he's determined not to be rolled over again. It's a clever ploy, but by keeping the maximum strain on he'll be forced to come right round into the bank. He gives it up and I can gain a few more yards as he turns and wallows. One more churning dive away and in he comes, zig-zagging and flailing over the net.

A glittering, perfect example of a common carp, and if I'm not mistaken, a couple of pounds heavier than my first guess. There you are, exactly 12½lb. You won't catch many bigger than that here, though I've seen one that looks as if it might go to 20. My best is 13¾, and I once got smashed by a carp 2 or 3lb heavier. The beauty of this place is in the actual quality of the fishing rather than the quantities of any outstanding fish. And, as you saw, the carp are cunning, powerful and exquisitely beautiful. All this at a pool with such classical attributes, and you can't be less than a happy angler. As far as I'm concerned, you're only successful if you're happy.

So that's the demonstration over, and my confidence restored. Now, with the sun just beginning to curve behind the oaks and the breeze just beginning to sink towards the evening stillness, we'll creep back to where we threw out the pigeon peas. There's always a chance that the spooked carp will come back to this reed bed and start taking non-submersible again, but I think it's wisest to vacate a pitch for at least half an hour after you've landed a fish.

Nothing in the first baited pitch. Nor the second. Third time lucky. It looks as if a cow's been wallowing in the margins. Great clouds of disturbed mud, some of the clouds – look there, to your left – still visibly billowing. Keeping well out of sight, because they're obviously right under our noses, I'll toss in another handful of bait and then, without any request for hard cash, lend you my rod. You could float fish for them; that would be fun – there's nothing to beat a float for excitement when it mysteriously slides away into the carp haunted depths (break here while we watch a kingfisher dart low across the pool). Personally, though I love float fishing, I'd be tempted to go straight in here without messing about. I'm glad you agree, I'd start hopping about with frustration if I had to watch you retackling with all those fish truffling about for our bait. I sometimes blow a fuse simply by tying on a new hook and it staggers me that anglers can use rigs that are so complex they have to refer to a diagram. Perhaps these people exist in a different time zone to me; I'd just explode if I had to spend longer than three minutes tackling up.

That's it, two field beans nicked on with the point of the hook just under the skin, but not penetrating into the hard kernel. Just a couple of rod-lengths out will do, and another little handful directly over the hook-bait. Close the reel pick-up and just lay the rod over your knees.

It's going to be a perfect summer evening. The breeze has dropped altogether, the pool is like a mirror, the sky is clear, the birds are enthusiastic about everything, the air smells of sun-baked grass and water-mint — and *there*, even as I'm droning on, your line is beginning to tighten...

4
CHUB
by Arthur Clarke

It has been said by those that study the evolving character of man that the primeval urge to hunt has remained as strong in certain individuals as ever it was in prehistoric times. Though this urge manifests itself in many different forms in every aspect of contemporary life, it is my belief that in the field of angling it results in the individual becoming a specialist chub fisherman.

Not for him the trance-like coma induced by protracted contemplation of a brightly-painted but stationary float. He finds his salvation in shallow clear running streams where the quarry can be viewed in its habitat, in the tailoring of his methods to suit the occasion and in the silent unseen approach of the predator that hunts alone.

This is not to say that the true chub fisherman is easy to recognise, for he comes in many guises: from the extrovert Midland 'townie' who, once on the riverbank, merges in as if planted there, to the silent country dweller who will refuse to fish if another angler settles down within a mile of his chosen swim. Their only common ground is the urge to catch chub.

The consistently successful chub fisherman is a man of versatility and imagination. He will be found fishing in all weathers and at all times of the day and night using a variety of methods and baits unequalled in any other field of angling. His approach is always flexible and he arrives at the water with no preconceived idea or rigid formula for the catching of chub.

Of course it is quite possible to catch chub, especially in the bigger rivers, by aping the match angler; feeding a swim and trotting a waggler down the middle. But this is not true chub

Playing big chub in fast water requires powerful tackle.

fishing. This method will catch anything that comes along and the angler is failing to demonstrate any true understanding of the fish he is catching. When the specialist chub angler sets out to catch chub he wants to catch chub and nothing else, and the methods, tactics and baits he uses are purposely selected to do just that.

The river chub is a true wild creature, born and bred with all the instincts and reflexes that nature provides and owing nothing to man. In his initial years his shoaling instinct is strong to provide protection against the attack of predators. But as he matures and his size increases the instinct lessens and he becomes more solitary. He may live as part of a group of similar-sized fish in areas that suit him, but he will no longer exhibit true shoal behaviour.

Spawning time, often said in angling books to be as early as February, in fact takes place much later, usually in late May, and sometimes as late as July. Early season will find him in poor condition; sometimes the males have head tubercles and often exhibit bloody patches on the flanks. Females grow much larger than males, mature later and live longer. Chances are that all big chub are female and few males will exceed 3lb in their lifetime.

The main diet of chub obviously varies from river to river, but it would appear that vegetable matter in the shape of weed forms the bulk of their food. Nymphs, caddis, beetle larvae, molluscs, shrimps and water bugs have all been found in the stomach of chub, with the addition of small fish in the larger specimens. Of course on heavily-fished waters the diet will include a proportionately greater amount of angler's bait.

The eyesight of the chub is keen and much of his food is located during daylight hours using this sense. He is, like the trout, a food interceptor and likes nothing better than to station himself in or close to a flow, and pick out any edible-looking titbits that come down. During coloured water conditions and at night time his very powerful olfactory sense will take over and he will venture some distance actively searching for food rather than letting it come to him. Water temperature has less effect on feeding than most other species but bad water conditions will see him off the feed for some time. The very worst conditions for chub on my local rivers are during high water caused by snow run-off, especially if local authorities have salted nearby roads. As the water subsides, though, and clean water works its way downstream then the chub feed with a vengeance, and it's during these conditions that the best bags are taken.

During the summer months and the low, clear conditions that usually occur, chub will feed all day and night, but it takes a good angler to catch them consistently. It is at this time, April to October, that the chub gains most weight. With the abundance of natural food available and the need to stock up before the leaner, colder months his tastes become extremely catholic and it is hard to find a bait that the chub will not take rather than one that he will. Heavy angling pressure will to some extent tailor his menu but the inventive angler will have little difficulty in finding something that the chub will eat.

The subject of baits for chub is a vast one and almost anything edible has some potential. My own experience suggests, though, that the chub does not have a sweet tooth like the carp and prefers a more savoury diet. Some recent experiments with flavoured pastes

Laying on after dark in the winter can produce some chub.

resulted in few fish to those baits that relied on sweeteners for effect, but a far greater number fell for meat and fish flavours.

Natural baits are far more plentiful during summer and the keen chub man will find that the time spent collecting them will be repaid many times. Crayfish, minnows, bullhead, loaches and elvers are all effective baits but become harder to find year by year. On the other hand slugs, wasp grubs, immature fish, beetles and grasshoppers will all take chub if presented in the correct manner.

The old favourite of bread in its various forms, cheese and cheese paste, maggots and worms will continue to take chub on waters not subjected to too great an angling pressure, but on those that are their effectiveness will lessen with time. It may be that, as has happened with carp, a chub bait revolution is just around the corner. Certainly more chub anglers seem to be experimenting with carp-type baits and results in some areas are encouraging. For my own part, and as a keen early summer carp fisherman, I have tried various flavoured pastes, some commercial 'boileys' and a number of particles, all with rather mixed results.

Paste based on trout pellet took a number of chub (and barbel) after prolonged prebaiting, and I suspect that if it was used more would see better catches made on it. High nutritive value (HNV) pastes without flavouring were taken with caution, rather I suspect because of their light colouring and resemblance to bread than any other reason. Flavoured and dyed pastes fared slightly better, with the single exception of highly-sweetened pastes which failed completely. The experiments with 'boileys' is still proceeding and I think that a much greater exposure to them is needed before good results will be seen.

Particles have yielded even more mixed results. A prebaiting scheme using hemp and aimed primarily at barbel resulted in few chub being taken despite the swims containing more chub than barbel. Sweetcorn fished over hemp resulted in more chub, basically, I believe, because of its greater visibility. Other mass baits such as red dari seed and tares were a complete flop and it is my impression that chub, unlike other members of the carp family, are extremely reluctant to act as piscatorial vacuum cleaners.

My conclusions from all this experimenting with baits are of course by no means conclusive, and a scientist would have rejected my uncontrolled methods out of hand. But they satisfy me in that on the rivers I fish chub will pick up a stationary bottom-fished bait only if it is 'visible', i.e. can be detected by the senses of sight or 'smell'. They will almost never investigate baits that are not immediately attractive to either of these senses. Moving baits are different in that the period of investigation of the edibility of the bait is usually shorter if the fish is to retain its station in the swim. This can result in a take on bait that would not be even looked at if statically ledgered. Paradoxically, baits that took chub when statically ledgered were not very successful when trotted but these were mainly baits of a non-buoyant nature such as pastes and 'boileys' which are difficult to present in a natural way on the move.

The tastes of chub narrow during winter as a result of a slowed metabolic rate and the decreased range of natural food available. This is to a certain extent reflected in their reluctance to take some baits that they will jump at during the warmer months. Luncheon meat, always a good summer bait, has brought me little reward in a swim where chub were quite willing to take cheese paste all day long. Preserved or fresh fish baits and frozen crayfish were similarly

A summer dawn and Arthur Clarke ledgers a traditional chub raft.

unsuccessful, yet at this time I was able to take small chub on floating plugs fished in the same way.

All in all, the bait situation is as open as ever and there will always be the question in the chub fisherman's mind, 'Shall I stick to the old and tested favourites or experiment with something new?' For myself I will continue to experiment.

Probably more has been written in the last few years about the location of chub than any other angling subject, with the single exception of carp. Richard Walker's tenancy on a stretch of the Upper Great Ouse (which I was many times privileged to fish) possibly sparked off the enormous interest in small river chub which resulted. Unfortunately it has also led to enormous fishing pressure on those stretches of other rivers which resembled the famed Great Ouse fishery.

Dick's writings accurately pinned down the swims where we could reasonably expect to find chub, and to a certain extent his advice is as good today as it was in the 1960s. The overhanging vegetation, undercut banks etc still, in many cases, contain their population of chub. But on those waters that are experiencing increased angling pressure these swims often become depopulated, as more and more fish suffer the indignity of being caught. It is then up to the angler to rediscover the new swims. On my local rivers the result is a general movement of chub into more open water and the creation of a roving population. Whereas in the past it was possible to fish the same chub over and over again, it would now appear that this no longer happens. On occasions the swims are entirely depopulated and the chub nowhere in evidence. Exceptions do occur, such as the long smooth glide with a reed mat on the far (private) bank which cries out to be trotted with traditional Avon-type tackle. This has had its population of chub since the early 1960s when I first fished it, and still does. But those 'banker' swims where a ledgered bait worked under the branches always produced bites now no longer give up their fish to order. Not always because the fish are more wary, but often because there are no longer any fish there.

Another problem that has occurred with increased angling pressure is the 'backing away syndrome'. When the river was comparatively unfished the chub tended to hook themselves on ledgered tackle. The way in which they took the bait ensured that this would happen irrespective of the rig used. A fish would first mouth the bait as if testing it for edibility and sometimes causing a small nod

This 3-pounder engulfed a 2-inch crayfish.

of the rod tip. If it was satisfied with the bait it would then turn downstream with the bait between its lips producing a tremendously fast 'pull round' and setting the hook in the process. This type of bite is becoming a rarity as the defensive mechanism of the chub evolves. The angler is nowadays more likely to experience a slow 'pull round' after the initial rounding but on striking will find he has missed what appeared to be a perfect bite. If the bite is left to 'develop', usually nothing happens, and the angler is left to recover an unmarked bait. From observations it would appear that the chub are picking up the bait as before, but instead of turning downstream they now *back* downstream with the bait held daintily in the lips for a distance of about 2ft and then turn round and away. If the resistance of the rod or quiver tip is felt they immediately release

A small chub taken on an artificial cranefly.

the bait while a strike tears it out anyway. My, albeit clumsy, solution to this was to allow the fish plenty of slack line by means of a bite indicator between reel and butt just balanced against the stream. This resulted in more fish hooked from heavily-fished swims, so long as the bobbin movements were ignored and the pull round on the quiver used to trigger the strike.

Daytime fishing during the summer is very often a matter of visual location on the small clear waters I love to fish, but an old trick can often be used to pinpoint individual fish. A few crusts thrown onto the surface and allowed to float down will usually evoke some sort of reaction from feeding chub (small dace and seagulls too!). They may not actually take the crusts, especially if this method has been done to death anyway but subsurface swirls and bow-waving will often give away the position of good fish. The angler must then get himself into position to fish without further informing the chub of his presence. This usually involves a fair bit of creeping and crawling about in the undergrowth, and it's a fact that the best chub usually come from the least accessible swims. Few anglers remember, however, that it is possible to fish upstream, and there is usually less chance of being seen from a downstream approach. Heavy natural baits such as slug and crayfish can be cast easily with no extra weight on the line and the current used to bring the bait to the notice of the intended victim.

On occasions chub will snap at a bait that lands with a splash close by. I think this is a reflex action and very big, difficult-to-tempt chub often fall for it. Slug is one of the best baits for this method, but a hook full of cockles or pieces of swan mussel is just as effective if slugs are difficult to obtain during dry periods. Baby frogs are also said to be good but any conservation-minded angler should give these a miss.

Crayfish are becoming scarcer as rivers become more and more polluted with agricultural chemicals, but there is still little to beat them during hot low water conditions. My local rivers still contain a few but several of the gravel pits that line the river now have a thriving population and these can be caught with a landing net and a torch on the shallow gravel beaches at night.

Crays are generally fished freeline to known fish. They sink slowly and should be worked in little jerks rather like a plug. Do not strike immediately you get a take, especially if the cray is a large one; give the chub several seconds to get a good hold. Crayfish should be killed before use and hooked with a large hook through the second segment from the tail in an upwards direction. Large crays may be too heavy to cast and should have the claws removed to lighten them. Do not take crays for bait that have egg clusters hanging from the body. They should be returned to the water to breed.

Fly fishing for chub seems to be a waste of time on my local rivers, and although small chub and dace are taken the bigger fish are very wary of heavy fly line. I expect that a trout fisherman used to small rivers and possessing all the skills that that type of fishing demands would fare better than me. I have done better with flies fished on coarse tackle using a controller (bubble float), and once took three chub over 4lb on artificial craneflies using this method. I believe, however, that there are other more effective methods the angler can use, and now only resort to flies when the chub are obviously feeding on them.

Summer night fishing for chub can be very exciting, and although demanding a fair amount of tackle handling skill will often be the only time when the really big chub on a stretch become vulnerable. During the bright nights of early summer the chub is still locating baits by sight and surface-fished baits are a viable proposition. Floating crust in particular is easily seen silhouetted against the sky, and chub that would ignore this bait during the day will often fall for it after dark.

Static ledgering, though, is the method usually chosen with all the usual swims producing fish. Make sure you know your way about on the bank before attempting this sphere of summer chubbing, especially if there is a chance of early morning mists. More than one experienced angler has had problems in this situation.

By the onset of winter the chub has fully recovered from spawning exertions and is a different fish from his early season character. The rich feeding of summer has packed on weight and muscle, improving his fighting ability and sharpening his wits.

During autumn the chub can be in an awkward feeding mood as the colder weather causes a slowing-down of the metabolism. Sometimes he will feed with abandoned caution, especially after a flush of heavy rain has cleared away much of the dying weed and leaves. At other times he will refuse almost everything you can offer and leave the angler wondering what was wrong with his tackle/bait/approach or whatever else he can blame.

With the dying-away of the weed it becomes more viable to fish a moving bait, and the traditional and deadly method of long trotting

Big bags of chub can be taken from a single swim by adopting long trotting tactics.

Chub fishing on the river bank during a cold spell.

can be practised. This involves long-range float fishing enabling the angler to distance himself from the scene of the action, so taking many more fish than shorter-range methods would permit. Stretches suitable for this type of fishing should be reasonably straight with an even flow and a flattish bottom. The depth is not so important, but if chub-holding features line the banks then all the better.

The basic idea of long trotting is, by groundbaiting, to draw the chub into an area far enough away from the angler so that casting, playing and landing the fish can be performed without scaring the feeding shoal. This should be some 20–25yd downstream of the chosen fishing position, but in clean water the further the better.

Concealment is important when fishing clear rivers for specimen fish.

Groundbait, which should be samples of the hookbait, should be thrown into the swim so that it arrives about 6in above the bed at the place where you wish the shoal to collect. On slow-flowing waters this can be difficult to achieve without the aid of a catapult or a strong throwing arm.

Tackle should consist of a light but stiffish float rod, a reel capable of feeding out line smoothly (a centrepin is ideal), line of 3 or 4lb BS and hook sizes to suit the bait being used. In swiftish currents it pays to have a landing net with a large mesh (see Fig. 10). Micromesh can make it difficult to use one-handed, and until quite recently I had to use an old knotted net to land fish comfortably. Thankfully large-mesh non-knotted nets are now available.

If you plan to retain your catch for photographing, try to place the keepnet where the current will not flatten the fish against the bottom of the net or scales will be lost and the fish suffer.

Retaining control of float tackle at longish ranges is only achieved by practice, but the beginner will find it easier if he starts off using a biggish Avon-type float that takes 3 to 4 swan shot. The shotting pattern should be arranged so that the bait has plenty of free movement with initially no shot less than 18in from the hook. The depth should be set deeper than the water and the float not allowed to rove freely down the swim but held back so that the bait precedes

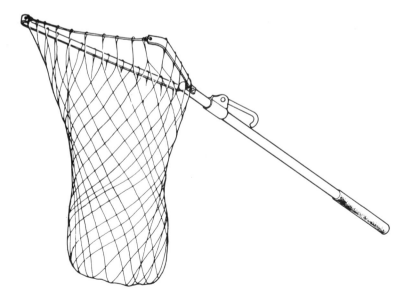

Fig. 10 A 32in apex landing net with telescopic handle.

A brace of summer chub taken on floating crust.

it. Recovering the tackle after an unsuccessful trot should be performed as close to the near bank as possible and out of the main trotting line.

Feeding the swim should be on the principle of light and often and always placed to arrive at the same place 6in above the bottom. If a fish is hooked it should be brought upstream away from the feeding area as quickly as possible and played out under the rod tip. Unfortunately this can sometimes prove difficult with the bigger fish, especially if they open their mouths as they are being brought upstream. Chub have big mouths and in a strong current it acts rather like a windsock with no hole in the downwind end. A terrific strain can be put on the tackle which can only be alleviated by steering the fish in towards the bank and out of the main flow.

If bites are found to be occurring further and further upstream, concentrate the next few handfuls of feed further downstream until the fish drop back again and the distance is maintained.

However light your rod, it is inevitable that a sore arm will result from long periods of trotting. I developed a bad case of tennis elbow one year until I learned to take a break every hour or so, but even these rest periods can be put to good use. Slide the float a couple of feet up the line and cast well downstream. Lay the rod in a couple of rests and sit back, have a smoke, eat your sandwiches or just twiddle your thumbs. Every few minutes chuck a handful of feed in until you are ready to trot again. Often the best fish of the day will be taken in this way.

When I was younger I used to chub fish throughout the winter at every opportunity. Bad weather or water conditions didn't influence me, and although I learnt a lot about chub the number of blank sessions were discouragingly high. On my local river, where the levels and flows are determined by the whims of the automatic sluice gates, it is often difficult to judge what conditions will be at any given time. A close study of the action of the sluices and how they respond to rain and drought cut down the number of sessions and lessened the chances of blanks. Prolonged sessions taught me the type of swim that fished best under given conditions and I was able, after a time, to predict where I would be most likely to catch a fish or two. Often the best periods turned out to be at night, and weather notwithstanding I fished a lot of sessions through the night during the coldest months. Results showed that there is little point in fishing after midnight unless the weather is exceptionally mild and the water in perfect condition, i.e. normal level and 'smoky'

Chub fishing on the River Avon at Downton.

colour. I fished both open water as well as traditional chub swims and did as well in both. Under exceptionally cold conditions or high water the traditional swims had the edge over the open water, but even then the better fish still seemed to come from the latter. The absolute killer was snow water run-off laced with road salt, and I would advise any keen chub angler to give these conditions a miss.

I have said little in this chapter about stillwater chub because, with one exception, they do not seem to grow big in my local waters. The exception is a tiny pit which was stocked with a few large chub some years ago. John Wilson took a 6lb 7oz fish from it, but this does appear to be the only chub to have attained any great weight in a still water in this water. Because of my lack of experience in this sphere of chub fishing I must leave writing about them to anglers who have fished for and caught them.

I have little doubt that the next record chub will come from a still water but, if and when it does, I for one shall be sorry. To me the chub is a running-water fish, an inhabitant of clear fast streams, and fishing for it in gravel pits is a different game altogether.

5
EEL
by Trevor Housby

Eel fishing is not everyone's idea of good fun. Those that know and understand serious eel fishing find it a fascinating occupation. To most anglers, however, their knowledge of eels is limited to the bootlace variety which invariably swallow the hook right down before turning the lure into a slime-filled ball that is impossible to untangle. Even true eel fanatics dislike small eels; for them the search is always for big eels of say 4lb and upwards. The problem with big eels, however, is basically location. Most waters hold eels, but few contain big eels, so specialist eel-anglers normally fish lakes, reservoirs and occasionally canals. Some rivers probably hold the odd huge eel, but the problem is to avoid the many small eels that continually worry baits intended for better fish.

Despite many years of serious eel-fishing I am still amazed at the unexpected places where big eels get caught. A tiny brick pit might well hold monster eels, whereas a nearby lake which to all appearances could produce specimens simply does not come up to scratch. A huge eel close to 7lb in weight was found still alive in the Serpentine lake in Hyde Park. This fish was choking on a hefty roach and could have made its way into the lake via the London drainage system. To my knowledge, however, no one has ever eel-fished in the Serpentine to find out whether this water contains other eels similar or larger in size.

Only recently I was granted permission to fish in a large ex-gravel pit, now turned trout water, to discover what stocks of coarse fish it contained. It was known to hold perch, pike and tench but little else. To make things easier I was allowed to take a friend with me, two for use with float-fished maggots and the other for use with a deadbait, in this case sardine. At the point we chose to fish, the bank dropped directly into 8ft of water. Having groundbaited with maggot we settled in to wait for fish to find one or other of the baits. Within minutes, sheets of large bubbles came frothing up from the depths. These showed that fish had found the loose maggots but from the bubble size I was sure they were not tench. During the next hour we caught ten eels between us on maggot. **Not one eel weighed less than 2½lb and several were close to 4lb. We also caught one solitary tench of an estimated 2lb weight.**

The live and deadbait rods had not twitched throughout this activity so we decided to move them further along the bank. Seconds after I cast out a live minnow my float bobbed twice, then slowly disappeared under the surface in classic perch style. Striking was merely a matter of lifting the rod. As I did so, something extremely large and angry sent up a huge gout of disturbed mud and weed. Then it turned and swam at high speed out into the lake. I realised instantly that it was not a perch. It was too fast and far too strong. As the fish tore off I decided that I had hooked a biggish pike. I was not using a wire trace and I expected the fish to chew through the light nylon. For some reason this did not happen, and as I began to gain line I started to think seriously about the possibility of bringing the fish to the net.

The water in this pit is permanently cloudy and I hadn't had a sight of the fish since the struggle began. Slowly but very definitely the fish was slowing down enough for me to regain most of the lost line. Soon it was almost directly under the rod tip sending up clouds of thick mud from the pit bed. Gradually it began to lift and as my companion stood by with the big net the fish surfaced. Instead of a pike we found ourselves looking at an immense eel. Not only was it very long, it was also very thick in the body. An eel to end all eels. The magical monster that most eel men dream about and don't have the good fortune to hook. I actually had its head over the net frame when the chafed line parted against its teeth. Instantly it shot backwards and vanished for ever.

Neither of us came to put a weight on that eel. I had caught eels up to an ounce under 7lb and my mate had caught fish to 6lb. This lost eel dwarfed all our previous fish. In later sessions we had fish to exactly 5lb from this trout pit but we never saw or set hook into the big one again. Why this fish should grow to such a large size in this pit no one could say, but whatever it was it suited them, for all the

Trevor Housby with a specimen freshwater eel caught on lobworms.

the idea being to fish two rods each: one baited with live minnow, fish we caught gave the impression of being comparatively young.

For those anglers who have never tried serious eel fishing, and are undecided on just what sort of water to start on, my advice would be:

1) Listen to local angling gossip. If you hear about a big eel being caught or lost then that particular water is worth trying.
2) Avoid any water which holds lots of small to medium-sized eels.
3) Look for the prison-type water. By this I mean a lake or pit with no true outlet and steep sides. Small eels can usually find their way into this sort of water but may be unable to leave it to make their spawning migration. When this happens the fish simply stay 'locked in', growing larger and larger until they finally die of old age. There is a very old gravel pit near my Hampshire home that conforms exactly to this prison water description. The only practical way into the pit is via a 6-in pipe that projects from the bank some 10ft above the pit surface. This pipe carries the inflow water from a nearby stream allowing immature eels instant access to the pit. There is, however, no outlet other than natural seepage. This means that all eels entering the water are totally trapped. To my certain knowledge this pit has produced eels to 9lb plus plenty of 5–7lb fish. This is living proof of the prison water theory. If you have a similar water in your locality you could easily discover that you have equally large eels in a captive situation. Big eels are never truly common and it may take many blank sessions before the first one is caught. On the pit I have just described, the average catch rate is one eel to every four or five blank sessions.

EEL TACKLE

To the best of my knowledge there is no rod yet designed for eel fishing. This could well change in the future, for with the popularity of eel fishing spreading I am sure someone will come up with a custom-built rod for the job. The majority of eel anglers use pike or carp rods for their eeling. Rods with a test-curve of 2–2½lb make first-class eel rods. This may sound heavy for use against fish which seldom top the 6lb mark, but as any successful big-eel man will tell

An eel caught on minnow.

you a big 'slimey' fights harder than most fish twice or three times its size.

One of the keenest eel anglers I ever knew was Maurice Johnson, who was an original member of the now long disbanded Hampshire Specimen Group. Maurice fished only for eels. His tackle was a light beach caster and large fixed spool loaded with 20lb BS braided line; this was unbelievably heavy gear for freshwater angling, but, as he said when he finally hooked a monster, he wanted tackle with guts enough to drag it in as quickly as possible.

That was, of course, in the days of glass rods. Modern carbon or boron rods do the job just as well, possibly even better. The 2 or

2¼ test rods can be fished with lines of up to around 17lb, strong enough to stop most eels in their tracks. Some of the largest lines, in particular the Drennen double strength, are so fine in diameter that they lend themselves perfectly to big-eel fishing. There are now so many good patterns on the market that the angler is totally spoilt for choice. I still use a pair of old but trustworthy Mitchell 300s for eeling. If I changed them I would probably purchase a pair of the rear drag pattern reels.

Most of today's anglers prefer to backwind on a running fish, but I prefer to use the clutch system of the reel, and a clutch that can be operated from behind the reel is preferable by far to one that has to be adjusted via a tension nut on the face of the spool. There is nothing new about rear drag pattern reels; they originally emerged in the late 1950s in the shape of the ABU 444 and the Sportex. Both these reels failed at that time to meet with public approval and were phased out accordingly.

Today the stern drag reels have reappeared and found instant approval with the modern specialist anglers. Eel tackle is invariably simple. For short-range work the weight of the bait is normally sufficient for casting purposes. Lead can be added as required should longer casting be necessary. One of the major breakthroughs in recent years is the new chemically-sharpened hook. Several companies now market these and so far I can find no fault with them.

LOCATING EELS

Like all large fish, eels have favoured areas. It may even be that large eels are to a degree territorial. Certainly an area which holds a big eel seldom produces a bootlace. Big eels are cannibals and any small eel which enters their territory is probably killed and eaten. I have long held a theory that most big eels are found in close proximity to the bank. Occasionally in a situation where an island area or a specific snag is thought to hold eels I indulge in long-range fishing, but for the most part I much prefer to fish the margins. My ideal eel swim is where the bank drops abruptly into 6–8ft of water. This is typical of many gravel pit swims where earlier digging operations have left a yard-wide submerged ledge which then drops off into deep water.

My preference is to fish the side facing the prevailing wind, the

A big catch of daylight eels caught on maggots.

theory being that the years of water slap have eroded the underside of the marginal ledge leaving many dark sheltered holes of the type favoured by large eels. This conveniently provides shelter, and the fact that most natural food is thickest in the margins allows the resident eels to live without exerting themselves.

I was once fortunate enough to be in a position to monitor visually the activity of a number of eels, some of which exceeded 7lb in weight. For the greater part of the day these eels stayed in their holes with just their heads poking out. Occasionally, when a shoal of small fry passed, the eels would slither partially out of their holes, snatch a little fish and slither back. I spent several days actually watching these eels without attempting to fish for them, and at no time did I see eels actively leave their holes and cruise off in search of food. I realise that at night this colony may well have become fully activated, but I doubt it. They were in a totally isolated and undisturbed area and the constant passing of small fry provided them with ample food supplies.

This unique opportunity to study eels took place in southern Ireland on the old Royal canal outside Mullingar. This section of the canal had been disused for many years and the locks had fallen into total disrepair. The bottom of each lock was a paved area formed of huge stone slabs. Originally each slab had been cemented to the next. Now most of this cement had worn away, leaving huge cracks which provided the big eels with perfect resting places. The interesting thing was that each eel was a monster. The smallest looked to weigh around 5lb, and the largest was on or over the double-figure mark.

I discovered this eel colony while walking the towpath in search of giant rudd. Having spotted it, however, I forgot all about rudd and became obsessed with eels. I quickly discovered that if disturbed the eels drew back inside the crevice. This made me think that below the paving the water had hollowed out a considerable hole. At that time I was in Ireland with Ron Barnett of carp and pike fame. Between us we began to plot the downfall of these eels, in particular the biggest one. We decided that to get to grips with the eels we would have to drop out baits actually through the cracks or down into the hole beneath the lock cutting.

Ron had a brand new stepped-up carp rod. This was in the days of split cane, and the rod constructed by Bob Southwell was the finest that money could then buy. I had a similar but slightly shorter rod of equal power. Terminal tackle was made up of 20in of

25 BS wire. The line was 15lb BS Danyl and the hook was a size 2 Model Perfect, humpy gear by any standards, but hopefully strong enough to drag the eels out of their holes.

For bait we decided on a bunch of big worms. I was the first to try, and the second my worms dropped through the crack I had a take that just about ripped the rod out of my hands. Full rod pressure, however, took its toll and a big eel shot out of the hole and tore off down the canal with me following it. This one weighed 5lb 14oz, probably the smallest of the bunch.

Ron tried next and exactly the same thing happened, except that this eel refused to come out. The hole under the slabs must have been huge, for the eel took line and raced around under the slabs. Ron tried everything. I have never seen anyone put so much strain on a rod. The eel didn't seem to notice. The constant wagging rod tip showed how active the fish was. Finally the line chafed through on the slab's edge and the eel-to-end-all-eels was gone. So, too, was Ron's rod. The cane fibres had shredded under the strain. The new rod was now so soft that it could never be used again.

It was now my turn again, and I was lucky that this eel reacted exactly like the first one. It later weighed in at 6lb 6oz.

Strangely, we never got another eel from that lock cutting. Nor did we see them again. Obviously eels learn quickly. I also learned a great deal about eel behaviour, a lesson which has stood me in good stead since that time. Normally when I eel-fish I decide on an area which I think is capable of producing eels. Once a swim is chosen I set up my stall well down the bank from the area to be fished. The bait or baits are then cast down along the bank to the actual swim. I **usually bracket a likely swim by using two rods each with a different bait. The first bait is dropped a yard or two off the bank. The second is cast further along and about 5yd out. The theory is that the close-in bait should draw the resident eel out of its hole. The second bait should be in a position to attract an eel that has been out hunting and is returning to its retreat.**

EEL BAITS
At a pinch eels can be caught on just about any bait, providing it is fresh. Barbel and chub anglers, for example, catch plenty of eels on cheese or tinned meat. For serious eel fishing, however, there are only three really effective baits.

1) Fish, used either alive or dead. Eels are active predators and will take small live fish readily. Small whole dead fish or sections cut from larger fish are extremely good. Eels are fussy feeders and in my opinion stale baits are a total waste of time. Even baits which have been caught and deep-frozen do not catch as well as truly fresh bait. Almost any freshwater fish make good deadbaits. My favourites, however, are tiny perch or medium gudgeon. Perch are probably the most productive of the two.

2) Worms, preferably large earthworms or lobworms, are highly-effective eel baits. On waters where there is a high percentage of small to medium eels, worms unfortunately produce far too many small fish. For this reason I only use worm bait on water known to hold only a few large eels.

3) A little-known but highly-effective eel bait is meat. The first time I saw this used was while fishing a Hampshire lake with Lymington angler Dave Fawcett. I was in fact carp fishing, but Dave decided on an eel in an adjacent swim. He had been unable to procure any dead fish and on impulse went to the local butchers. He purchased a quarter of fresh rabbit. This he cut into strips and, having cast out one rod, he turned to bait up the second rod when the indicator on the first rod hit the butt ring with a crash.

In all he caught a dozen eels before running out of bait. The smallest weighed about 1½lb. The largest topped 4lb. From that time on he used meat for all of his eel fishing. Being a part time gamekeeper, all manner of strange animals came his way. I know for a fact that he took large eels on squirrel meat and on a rat leg, back-up baits when he failed to buy or catch rabbits.

TIME OF DAY

Most anglers still assume that large eels are basically nocturnal feeders. On hard-fished waters this is probably true, but I have found that I can catch as many big eels during the day as at night. On well-fished lakes and pits the middle of a hot afternoon can often be productive. It is at this sort of time that I normally prefer to fish at long range. I do not think that the bankside eels move out; it is rather that the eels that live offshore become more active.

Bait is invariably dead fish, for I find that eels that live most of their lives away from the bank are almost exclusively fish-eaters. As always the reel spool is left open with the line tucked under a run clip. Eels are notoriously tackle-shy, dropping a bait at the slightest suspicion. Normally I find daylight eel runs are extremely definite affairs. At night large eels are obviously confident of the blanket of darkness that gives them shelter. This usually means that they eat the bait where they find it. During the day their habit is to pick up a bait and head for cover. The resulting run is usually a real 'screamer'. These fast runs are easy enough to strike at, for the eel seems to swallow or partially swallow the bait as it goes. My standard technique is to allow the eel to cover 10yd or more, then to close the reel pick-up, wait for the line to pull tight and lift the rod to set the hook.

Most eels are hooked just inside the mouth, which allows me to remove the hook and put the eel back in good shape. Like most anglers I prefer to return fish, although like most eel-men I get a few throat-hooked or even gut-hooked eels during a season. These I prefer to kill and have smoked.

EEL TECHNIQUES
Eel fishing is a simple style of angling, although some of today's anglers would have us think otherwise. Like most big fish, eels are greedy creatures which will only pass up an easy meal if something makes it suspicious. For meat, deadbait and worm fishing, straightforward ledger rigs are ideal. Leads should be either dispensed with or kept to the minimum size. I prefer to use all lead on a 6in line. This I believe helps to minimise the chance of an eel feeling any drag as it picks up the bait.

One or two eel anglers now use light dacron line as trace material. At present I am undecided on this. The idea is that nylon is stiffer than soft dacron and is more likely to alarm a taking eel. So far I have yet to prove this theory to my own satisfaction. Wire traces are definitely out as far as I am concerned. An eel's teeth are tiny although sharp. I find that a length of 12lb BS nylon makes a perfect trace.

Once hooked an eel should be bullied. Most eels are normally hooked close to home. To avoid losses in snags, holes etc the eel should be dragged out into more open water as quickly as possible, remembering that an eel can go backwards as well as forwards.

More than one monster eel has escaped by backing away, so forget all the niceties of playing your fish, and just concentrate on getting it to the net as quickly as possible.

6
PERCH
by Trevor Housby

The late Richard Walker once wrote that in his opinion a big perch was the most difficult of all British fish to catch. Having spent a good many years in search of big perch, I can only agree with him in this respect. Occasionally, of course, a water is found where big perch are caught regularly, but such places are rare and most anglers have to struggle to find and make contact with each specimen they catch.

My obsession with perch started by accident back in the mid-1950s at a time when perch were in fact more common than they are today. I was fishing the Thames below Old Windsor, basically for anything that came along. The day was hot and windless and the river looked flat and fishless, until an explosion of small fry indicated the presence of a predator. I had a few small gudgeon in my keepnet, one of which I used as livebait.

For over an hour nothing happened, then the tip on my home-built split-cane ledger rod pulled slowly round almost as though drifting weed had tangled in the line. Wrongly I assumed that this was what had happened, and it was not until I started to crank the reel handle that I realised that my gudgeon had been eaten by an obviously powerful fish. Minutes later, shaking with excitement, I slipped the net under a perch which weighed exactly 4lb 8oz, a monster by anyone's standards and a fish I have yet to equal despite many years of trying.

So the obsession began. Going big-perch-mad is easy, but finding the fish to sustain such an obsession is more difficult. For months I haunted the Old Windsor section of the Thames, but finally I realised that my first perch was going to be my last. From this

Dave Fawcett with perch of 2¼ and 2½lb, caught on deadbait from Hucklesbrook Lake near Fordingbridge.

venue big as the perch was it was obviously a one-off catch, a freak that would never be repeated. In those days, transport meant public transport or pushbike, and this put a limit to my area of possibilities.

The hot perch water at that time was Arlesey lake, Bedfordshire, a vast gravel pit which appeared to be fished by a handful of elite anglers. Time and again I read and re-read accounts by Richard Walker and John Nixon of expeditions to Arlesey. Lobworms were the in-bait, cast out into depths in excess of 60ft. How I lived those writings. The big fish hooked and lost in tangled cables and sunken machinery, the gut-tightening thrill of the first trickle of line leaving the reel spool. The imagined sight of big striped perch being pumped up through deep clear water. The despair that change of depth caused many of the big perch to blow out and die. All of this was heady stuff to a teenage angler with nowhere to fish and a desire for big perch.

Having read and very definitely digested everything Richard Walker wrote on perch, I formed a vision of the perfect perch water. What I had to find was a big gravel pit holding very deep water and with a known stock of perch in excess of 1½lb. I used this weight as a guide, for I had already noticed that so many waters contained millions of stunted perch but none larger than 4–6oz. I reasoned that any water that produced fish of 1½lb plus could easily produce a monster.

This supposition has stood me in good stead over the years since I first began my quest for specimen perch. By 'specimen' I mean any perch over 2lb in weight. A 2lb fish may not sound big, but in the case of perch I feel this is a good starting weight. The interesting thing about perch is the way they change their feeding habits as their size increases. Small perch are totally suicidal, snatching and swallowing any natural bait that comes their way. Even the most diminutive perch are predatory, taking livebaits almost as large as themselves. This trait continues until the perch reach a weight of 12–16oz. From then on the perch become cautious in the extreme, rejecting any bait that does not look and act naturally. Even on underfished waters the perch show the same cautious approach to a bait, and this makes life extremely difficult for the angler.

CHOOSING A PERCH WATER
Water selection is critical. One way of finding a good water is to 'keep your ear to the ground'. Match anglers, in particular, often discover perch before anyone else. I listen for any report of big perch taken or lost in local matches, then give the water a thorough going-over with conventional perch gear. Ninety per cent of all likely perch waters are man-made. Natural lakes seldom seem to produce big perch, possibly because most lakes are shallow in comparison to the average gravel pit.

I am convinced that extreme depths play an important part in the growth of perch. Comparatively new pits seem to be particularly productive where perch are concerned, and I am sure this is due to a limited original stocking of perch which have grown quickly on a diet of roach and, after a season or two, small perch. Such a water normally peaks within a 5–7-year period, by which time it is usually overrun by small perch while the original stock fish have died out in the natural progression of an advancing water.

Perch are prolific spawners. Despite predation by parent fish two or three seasons is enough to create a population explosion of tiny perch. Once this situation occurs the competition for food is such that few individual fish grow to any size. Once overrun by stunted stock, such a fishery can be written off the big-fish angler's list of potentially productive waters.

Although most gravel pits are large, smaller clay pits and brick ponds can also turn up trumps where big perch are concerned. What these waters lack in size, they normally make up for in depth, which is probably the most critical factor where perch growth rates are concerned.

Very occasionally a water will be discovered which has been stocked with giant perch which have been transferred from another water. There are two such waters in my local area, both having been stocked with huge perch trapped and netted from a nearby trout lake. Such waters should not be neglected. In my experience the newly-introduced perch seldom survive more than a few seasons so it pays to strike while the iron is hot.

WHEN TO FISH

Back in the Arlesey lake days, perch were regarded as very much of a winter species. The school of thought at that time was that in cold weather the normally separated perch packs took refuge in the deeper water. Being condensed into a smaller area naturally made them more vulnerable to the angler's baits. To a degree this is true. Winter perch are often found in limited sections of a lake. This, however, does not mean that winter is necessarily the optimum period for perch fishing.

In recent years I have come to realise that in many instances summer perch fishing can be far more productive than an average cold weather season. In the summer the fish can be expected to feed at any time of the day, whereas in the winter the feeding spell may come and go in less than an hour. The trick is to be able to differentiate between a summer perch swim and a winter one. High water temperatures mean that the perch tend to spread out and utilise virtually the whole lake in their search for food. Probably the least likely swims to produce are those swims which would normally fish well in icy conditions. Deep water holds little food during the summer months and the perch are well aware of this.

The secret of successful summer perch fishing is to locate the areas which perch habitually use as base camp. The idea is to present the bait in such a way that perch leaving or arriving at the holding ground are bound to see the bait en route. Man-made lakes seldom have even bottom contours. The passage of the digging equipment leaves gullies and ridges across the bottom.

The perfect perch swim in my opinion is on the edge of a shallow ridge where the water drops away into a medium-depth gully. One such place I fish regularly conforms exactly to my opinion of a

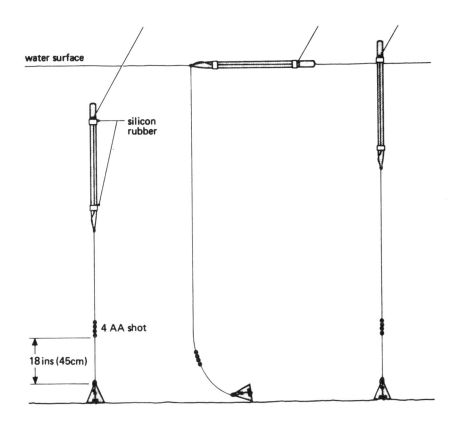

Fig. 11 Plumbing the depth.

perfect big perch swim. The gully is an average 8½–9ft in depth, while the ridge rises to within 3ft of the surface. On a clear day the sandy-coloured top of the ridge can be clearly seen from the bank, pin-pointing the swim exactly. A bait presented over this ridge will usually produce fish at almost any time of day. Sometimes a take comes within seconds of the tackle hitting the water; at other times a long wait is necessary. Sooner or later, however, the fish return to this swim, where they can be usually induced to take the bait.

During the winter this type of swim is usually a total waste of time. Mostly the perch are condensed into a small area which holds nearly 20ft of water, the deepest section of this particular pit.

I have made little practical reference to perch fishing in rivers or canals. Certainly big perch do exist in such places, but not in high enough numbers to interest the specialist anglers. To be successful with big perch on a consistent basis, gravel-type pits make the only realistic venues, unless you know of a natural lake which contains large perch. Reservoirs once produced plenty of good perch, but due to a particularly savage disease most reservoir perch stocks have long since been depleted. Gravel pits, which were also affected by this same disease, appear to be making a comeback, so maybe in time the reservoirs will also begin to produce big perch again.

One of the most interesting aspects of perch fishing in recent years has been the number of very big fish taken; by 'big' I mean 4lb plus. The odd thing is that in most instances all the fish have come from waters thought to be virtually devoid of perch. Where, then, have these fish been during their developing years, and why haven't they been caught in their immature stage? So far no-one has come up with an explanation for this sudden emergence of big fish.

PERCH FOOD AND THE MOST LIKELY BAITS FOR BIG PERCH

Perch of all sizes are opportunists. Just about anything that moves, crawls or swims in water is regarded as food by foraging perch. Some very big perch have also been taken on bread-based baits. Personally, however, I think these catches occur when a big perch attacks a shoal of small fish that are pecking at the bread bait, the bread being sucked in with a mouthful of feeding fry. To understand perch baits fully, it is essential to judge each productive bait on its own merit.

Worms
Richard Walker always favoured lobworms as the premier big-perch bait. This preference was, I believe, heavily biased towards its usage in the deep waters of Arlesey lake. Arlesey called for long-range fishing into extremely deep waters, two factors that made live fish bait impractical. The only bait likely to stay on during casting and stay lively after a high-speed descent into deep water was lobworm. Its success as a big-perch bait lay in these two factors, and the fact that it was the only bait used consistently in what was the country's finest big-perch water.

Personally, I have never favoured worms of any sort as perch bait. They certainly attract and catch perch, but irrespective of size they are far too vulnerable to the attentions of the smaller specimen. What is worse, most perch caught on worm swallow the bait and hook completely. This inevitably leads to a prolonged and messy abstraction which often results in a high mortality rate amongst the fish caught. Worms for me are no more than a standby bait when other more attractive baits prove unobtainable.

Deadbait
In recent seasons many very hefty perch have fallen to deadbait. Norfolk angler John Wilson is particularly adept at catching perch on dead fish, although by his own admission it is a bait that only works on certain waters. It would seem that perch will happily scavenge for dead fish on waters where suspended silt keeps visibility to a minimum. In clear water deadbaits just do not appear to hold perch appeal. On the disused gravel pits that I fish the clarity of the water is such that I have never yet had a take on a static deadbait. Small roach, rudd and perch make the best deadbait.

Livebait
Perch of all sizes are predatory. Even tiny 6-inch fish will attempt to eat other fish approaching their own size. It is only necessary to look at the huge mouth of say a 2lb perch to see that it is more than capable of swallowing 6–7-in fish. Perch are not only avid predators, they are also highly cannibalistic. My favourite big-perch bait is without question a small perch, the perfect size being 5–7in. A livebait of this size is immune to the attentions of small perch, but perfectly in keeping with a big perch's idea of the perfect meal.

At a pinch any other type of fish of similar size can be used as livebait, but in my experience perch livebait is invariably the best producer. Fish like minnows should not be used. Being small they attract far too many immature fish. Occasionally a very big perch will fall to a minnow but usually only when the bait is dropped right on its nose.

Depending on the nature of the water being fished, livebaits can be fished in a number of ways. Where snags or heavy weed abound, I find it pays to fish a tethered bait on a float paternoster rig. Over beds of thick bottom weed the baits can be fished under a float or on a free-roving principle. In both instances, the float should be kept as small and as streamlined as possible. In deep water or in areas where snags and weed are absent I find a ledgered livebait catches most fish. Big perch normally approach a livebait with great caution. For this reason I use a long tail between lead and hook which allows the bait to move freely at all times. Perch will drop any bait the instant they suspect all is not well.

Once a perch does decide to take a bait the bite is usually decisive. When large baits are used the fish should be given time to take the bait into its mouth. Unfortunately there are no set bite patterns, and most bites have to be judged by luck or experience. To make life easier for the angler and safer for the fish, treble hooks, even of the small barbless type, should never be used. My preference is for a size 6 or 8 barbless single hook to which a size 16 barbed hook has been wired, almost on the hair rig principle. The livebait can then be liphooked on the small hook leaving a larger hook clear. Even a throat-hooked perch can normally be removed safely from a barbless hook.

Maggot Bait

Maggots are not normally a bait associated with large perch. Oddly enough, however, big perch will often pick up a single or a bunch of maggots in preference to large worms or livebait. Maggots are particularly effective on waters that are hard-fished or totally unfished. On hard-fished waters the larger perch often become excessively line-shy, totally avoiding anything presented on a line of much more than 2lb BS. Under these conditions a good many perch are caught by match anglers, basically fishing fine small roach, rudd etc.

I have seen many big perch caught in this way, including a

A big perch caught on small perch livebait.

magnificent 3lb 14oz specimen caught by Poole angler Dick Anderton at Hucklesbrook lake. Dick was fishing during the closing hour of the match. The fish was probably attracted by the constant introduction of groundbait and hookbait samples plus the feverish activity of the feeding roach.

Caster (chrysalis) also makes a first-class perch bait. Unfortunately maggot-fishing for big perch normally means the angler must be prepared to catch an endless stream of small fish in the hope of finally contacting a big one. On lakes which hold limited fish stocks, but where big perch are known or thought to exist, maggot can be very effective. A natural dearth of small fish means that the resident perch must feed mainly on natural insects. Under these circumstances maggots can be extremely effective.

Only recently I fished this bait on just such a water. This pit, although large, holds very limited stocks of roach and perch, both species growing to large size. During an experimental netting session, perch to over 5lb were caught, weighed and returned. It was one of these giants that mopped up my maggots during a morning session on the water. This pit is dour on a good day and after two biteless hours I suspected I was in for yet another blank session. Then 20yd out my float lifted fractionally, sank again, then slowly began to move off towards the centre of the pit. The bite was slow and easy to hit.

What happened next was not so easy. The moment I struck, the fish changed into top gear and headed at high speed for a central island. Most big perch can be stopped fairly easily, but this one was different. Its fight style was typically perch-like: fast 10yd dash followed by a momentary pause and a second mad rush. Each time it accelerated, the clutch of my fixed spool screeched in anguish, while my long rod creaked under the strain.

Finally, as the fish started to turn, I lost contact. Initially I thought I had been broken up. When I reeled in, however, the hook was still attached, so obviously my strike must have set the hook into loose skin rather than solid fish. Of all the big perch I have ever hooked I have never encountered one with the weight or speed of this lost fish. I did not see it so I have no idea of its size. My impression was, however, that it would have weighed over 5lb.

Artificial Baits

Perch fall readily to various artificial lures although spinning is a method seldom seriously employed by perch anglers. Almost any small to medium-sized plug or metal spoon can be used, but I have always found either a small Mepps-type Bar spoon or a Toby-type nobbling spoon to be the most effective. The Toby spoon, being heavier and more streamlined, can be cast further and therefore covers more ground than any other type of lure. I have caught many perch of 2½lb plus on this type of spoon. I also lost one fish in the 4½lb range on it. Really big perch seem highly adept at shaking free of a hook, probably because the mouth skin of a big perch is paper-thin and tears easily under pressure.

Spinning is a method I use for short two-hour sessions on a water. For longer periods, I much prefer to bait fish. The beauty of spinning is that it enables me to travel light. One rod and a box of baits and swivels is all I need for a short session. The reason that spin fishing is so effective is because it allows the angler to cover a great deal of ground.

The static angler may fish all day in a 10yd-wide stretch of water. In two hours a spin fisherman can easily cover half an average lake.

Specialist angler Dick Anderton with a 3lb 14oz perch caught on maggots.

Perch take a lure solidly but gently, and most bites feel as though the spinner has snagged into bottom weed. The trick is to raise the rod tip at the slightest stoppage. If a perch is responsible the rod tip will give perfect indication of living movement and the angler can start to play his fish in a conventional manner. Takes often come seconds after the lure strikes the surface of the water; presumably perch see the spinner as a sick or damaged fish floating towards the bottom.

With one or two exceptions all my perch fighting has been done on lakes, pits and reservoirs. Of the three very different venues my natural preference is for disused gravel pits. Many reservoirs hold big perch, but sheer size alone makes such a water very difficult to fish. Gravel pits on the other hand rarely exceed 50 or 60 acres which makes fish location far simpler.

There was a period when I confined my perch fishing activities to the winter months only. This was due to the fact that just about everything published on big perch had stated that in cold weather the fish retreated to the deeper sections of a pit to live and feed in loose shoals. It took me a number of seasons to realise just how nonsensical this belief was. True, I caught some big perch by winter fishing in deep water but I also missed out on some of the hot periods of the summer season.

During my winter-only period I confined my activities to a number of large pits in the Thames Valley area. These waters produced well on occasion but success was often marred by a long string of blank sessions. Big-perch fishing is at best a slow occupation, and after a while I slipped into the numerous 'blanks' routine without thinking my fishing through. Looking back I realise that the rod hours involved were hardly compensated for by the catching of the odd fish. In those days rod hours were regarded as the maxim for ultimate success.

Later I realised that two hours spent at the right time was far better than many hours spent at the wrong time. This was particularly true of the winter months, when most bites occurred at the lightest part of the day. On one pit near Staines any take from a big perch came between 12.30pm and 1pm. Despite this I made a ritual of arriving before dawn and fishing on until full dark. Strangely enough my midday catches were often good and I took a number of fish to 3½lb.

Nick Putnam with a near 3lb perch taken on small perch livebait.

I was convinced that this water held perch in excess of the British record, a belief that was finally proved in a most dramatic fashion. The day started badly with a blinding snowstorm which made driving conditions very, very unpleasant. Finally, however, I arrived, parked and walked to my chosen fishing position. By this time the snow had stopped and the day gave promise of being bright, clear and very cold. I invariably use two rods for perch fishing, and with these set up and baited with strong little livebaits I settled back to watch my silver paper indicators for the slightest sign of a bite.

By mid-morning it became apparent that the pit was rapidly icing over and at midday I decided to give it best and head for home before the roads became iced over. I reeled in both baits, released the little fish as carefully as possible, then picked up my livebait can to release the dozen or so spare baits it contained. At the place I was fishing the water came up to the tops of my boots then dropped directly over a shelf to a depth of about 14ft. Once released the bait fish swam out and over the shelf to vanish into deep water.

A second later, they came dashing back to converge round my feet, as one of the largest perch I have ever seen cruised in magnificent splendour up out of the deep. This perch was totally uninterested in me, but very interested in the panic-stricken baits. If I had had one bait left in the can I could have caught that fish. But under the circumstances I could only stand and watch while it cruised up and down less than a yard from my feet. The sight of that fish kept me on that pit for another two winter seasons. Needless to say I never saw it again.

In my experience very big perch lead what can only be described as a charmed life. Practically every big-perch specialist has a fund of stories that relate to big fish, seen, hooked and ultimately lost. Many simply 'fall off' due to the hook hold tearing out. The strange thing is that most of the medium-weight fish in the 2–3½lb range stay on once hooked. One of the main loss factors can be put down to the fish's large mouth. A 4lb plus perch could easily eat an 8–10oz fish, and I believe that much of the angler's striking power is absorbed by the cavern-like mouth. To make matters worse, the skin inside the mouth is usually paper-thin, so thin in fact that it will tear easily under rod pressure. This causes the hook to fall out the second the fish gets an inch or two of slack line.

Most dedicated perch anglers use rods in the 1¼–1½lb test-curve range. Such rods do not have the softness necessary to maintain a solid hook hold. Big perch hooked during a match seldom come adrift during the fight. This, I am sure, is due to the flexibility of the average match rod designed for use with ultra-light lines. The problem is that match-type rods do not lend themselves to the sort of long-range work often necessary in perch fishing.

Certainly I favour softer glass rods for perch fishing. These may be old-fashioned when matched up to boron and carbon rods, but the glass will usually out-perform the more modern rods. I still own and use a pair of Davenport and Fordham rods designed by Peter Stone in the 1960s. So far I have yet to discover a modern rod which functions as well for perch fishing.

Having realised my mistake in confining my perch-fishing activities to the winter months, I now fish throughout the season. Because of this I have increased my knowledge enormously and caught a good many extra fish into the bargain. My winter experi-

Three big perch from a gravel pit, all taken on big baits.

ences had led me to believe that perch were basically a bottom- or near-bottom-feeding species. Once I began early-season fishing, I soon realised that perch are far more versatile feeders that adapt to whatever food is available, even to bouts of surface feeding.

On one occasion in the 1986 season I was fishing a Hampshire pit that was alive with tiny perch fry. To the left of my swim was a raft of silk weed. Every few minutes a gout of fry would break through this weed raft, obviously chased by larger fish. For a while I watched in the hope of actually sighting the attacker. Then I saw a mouth forced up through the weed, as an obviously hefty perch sucked in the stranded fry. In the space of an hour I saw the fish take half a dozen fry in this way. Obviously the circumstances were unusual but it proved to me that a hungry perch can be extremely flexible in its feeding habits.

Another exploded myth is the 'deep is best' theory. Early-season perch will live and feed in water barely deep enough to cover their dorsal fin. I have taken some nice fish from shallow bankside swims which at one time I would have totally ignored.

Sadly, big perch are not widespread in this country. During the past twenty years many once-prolific perch waters have been totally wiped out by perch disease. Despite this, there are more big perch than most people suspect. Any water rumoured to have produced a big perch is worth a serious session or two. The results will prove conclusively that the big perch are big and comparatively plentiful. A big perch is not only a beautiful fish to catch and look at, it is also a fish to be truly proud of. I have had perch fever for more years than I care to remember, and I always dream about that elusive 5-pounder. One day, maybe, I will catch such a fish. Until then I still love every second of my perch fishing.

7
PIKE
by Mike Booth

'If you want to catch a big fish, you must be able to imagine yourself as that fish. I can enjoy being a carp basking under lily pads, or a trout rising at mayflies, in my imagination I can be a fat old chub, or a timid roach, or even a bristly perch; but I can't for the life of me be an evil-minded snaggle-toothed monster of a pike.'

The above quote comes from *No Need to Lie* by the late Richard Walker. I agree with Richard when he says, 'If you want to catch a big fish, you must be able to imagine yourself as that fish.' Unlike Richard, however, I can't see the pike as an 'evil-minded' creature; instead, like any other fish, it follows the two main instincts of survival and reproduction. I find it easy to imagine myself as a pike; after all, like Richard, I have been hunting fish for most of my life.

Living in Dorset, I'm fortunately blessed with quality and varied pike-fishing on my doorstep. Within a few miles of my home I have available to me the fast waters of the Hampshire Avon, the more gentle flow of the Dorset Stour, and a different variety of still-waters.

In order to get the best sport available I have endeavoured to get to know the different waters as well as possible, thus enabling me to make the most of my fishing time. Using the best tackle, the best techniques and the best bait is of little use if the angler is fishing the wrong water at the wrong time.

The successful pike angler is not necessarily the man with matching carbon rods or the man with the most up-to-date technique and exotic bait (although he probably has these things). He is the man who has given pike behaviour and habits a great deal of thought and has acquired the knack of being in the right place at the right time.

Throughout the chapter it is my aim to take you through my pike-fishing year, not only to show you the methods I use but also to give you an insight into the thought that goes into my fishing. Due to the pressure of work I am unable to fish the summer months, so my season does not really start until September. This month is usually spent really getting ready for the winter. I'll spend quite a number of trips bait-catching to get a good supply of live and dead coarse baits. Time is also spent going round fishmongers to stock up on sea baits; mackerel, herring, sprats, sardines and smelt all have their uses, and I hate going fishing without a good supply of each of them in the freezer box.

The quality of your bait is of the utmost importance, and every effort must be made to acquire the best bait possible. Livebaits attract pike by sight and vibration, so it is obviously important that your livebait is visible to the pike, and also that it gives off plenty of vibration. The more vibration given off by the bait the larger the area they will attract pike from.

Deadbaits attract pike by sight and the scent that they release. It is therefore important that your bait is as fresh as possible, because, again, a fresh bait will give out more scent and attract pike from a wider area. Once the pike has located the bait it is more likely to take it if it is of good quality.

Another thing I do in September is choose the waters I will be fishing in the coming year. Normally I choose four areas:

1) A shallow lake.
2) A deep gravel pit.
3) The Hampshire Avon.
4) The Dorset Stour.

All these waters contain 20-pounders and there is also an outside chance of a 30.

The reason I choose these waters is because they respond differently to weather conditions and time of year, and the pike feed at different times. This is of vital importance, because if I get an afternoon off work there is little point in fishing a water which only produces fish in the morning. The shallow lake is best for fishing from dawn to midday, the gravel pit seems to produce from 11am until about 3pm, and the two main rivers produce all day. The best chance of a really big fish, however, is undoubtedly last light.

The different waters respond to different methods and approach;

Landing a good pike. With a big fish, having someone else to handle the net can be a great help.

this gives my pike fishing a great deal of variety, which is of importance to me because I'd hate to spend a whole season fishing just one water. It's the constant changing from one water to another that keeps my mind active and my interest and dedication at a peak throughout the whole year.

During September and October really all my fishing is done on the two stillwaters, in particular the lake. The weather is normally fairly mild and settled which the water responds well to, and also later in the year the water gets hammered and I like to have a month with the water to myself. If there is a sudden cold spell I head for the gravel pit, as the pike which have been fairly well spread out head towards the deeper water where they are easier to locate. As the weather becomes mild again, the pike spread out all over the pit and I move back to the lake.

I don't tend to fish the rivers very much at this time of year as the Jacks seem to be very active and the large fish are hard to find. The river is still in summer conditions with low water levels and an abundant weed growth. The food fish are well spread out and the large pike tucked behind a weed-bed could be anywhere in the river. Large pike can and are caught from rivers at this time of year, but I consider my chances of contacting a 20lb fish better from a stillwater at this time of year.

As the season progresses and October becomes November the weather becomes far more changeable and I start to spend more time on the gravel pit. The lake, being relatively shallow, is very susceptible to changes of temperature, and the pike tend to keep their feeding to settled spells of mildish weather. On the other hand, the gravel pit is over 15ft deep in places, and the change in water temperature is more gradual; and as I said earlier low temperatures are not a bad thing in the pit because they tend to drive the pike off the shallows into the smaller area of deeper water where they are easier to find.

I still don't spend much time on the rivers as the summer vegetation is dying and unless we've had a couple of good floods the river bed is covered in decaying vegetation. This gives off gas which seems to put all species of fish off the feed. The Stour suffers more from this than the Avon because of the slower flow.

To locate pike in stillwaters, firstly you must trace the food fish. The easiest way to do this is to be at the water at either dawn or dusk; often at this time the wind is very slight and the surface of the water calm. The food fish show themselves by pimping on the

A magnificent 25lb pike in peak condition. This fish was taken on a dead grayling, favoured as a pike bait because of its herby smell.

surface; if you find this then nine times out of ten you have found your pike.

Other ways to locate pike include the following.

1) Find out the contours of the lake or pit by using a plummet or an echo sounder, or by obtaining maps which your water authority may possess. Once you have learned the nature of the lake bed, places to explore are areas of deeper water, places with a variance of depth, gulleys and drop-offs.
2) If the water you are fishing is match-fished, go along to the weigh in and see where the biggest weights come from.
3) Leap-frog around the pit until the pike are located.

On some stillwaters pike may remain in the same place for considerable lengths of time; on other waters the hot spot could well move several times a season. This could be due to movement of bait fish or due to intense angling pressure.

December and January are when I start to concentrate on the rivers. The cold weather and floods we normally experience have got rid of most of the weed and the rivers should be a couple of feet up on summer level, and running fairly clear. Pike can be caught in coloured water but the chances of catching a large fish are extremely slim. It is better to fish a stillwater under these conditions.

The very best time to hit a river is when it's fining down and has just started to run clear; the longer the river has been in flood the better sport will be when eventually conditions become good.

During the winter of 1984–85 the Stour was out of condition for about six weeks; the day it began to run clear I was fortunate enough to have a morning off work. The fish went absolutely mad and I caught thirteen in all including fish of 11lb 14oz, 13 lb 10oz, 16lb 3oz, 16lb 10oz, 17lb 2oz, 17lb 4oz and 24lb. Days like this are extremely few and far between, but they're good for the old confidence when they do happen.

Ideal weather conditions for my rivers are frosty starts turning into overcast days with a temperature of about 7 or 8°C. The pike will feed in sub-zero temperatures as long as it's been that cold for a few days. The conditions I don't like for river piking are the nice still, warm, sunny spring-like days we sometimes experience towards the end of the season. These are very nice and comfortable days to fish, which is a good job because you won't catch much.

On the stillwaters I tend to use deadbaits far more than livebait.

On the waters you fish it might be different, but on my waters deadbaits seem to attract a far larger class of fish. For most of my deadbaiting I fish my baits freelined, but on occasions I suspend them off the bottom. Corpse baits can be fished in conjunction with a small bomb or several swan shot and air injected; sea baits are fished on a very simple sunk paternoster rig (see Fig. 12).

What I like about the rig is the fact that it is so quick to change from freelined to a paternoster set-up. The paternoster set-up is ready made up and kept on a winder, and to attach it to the freelined bait you simply clip it to the swivel of the trace via the link swivel at the top of the paternoster link.

You will no doubt notice that when the pike runs with the bait it will also have to drag the lead behind it; however I don't feel that this little bit of resistance will cause the pike to drop the bait.

Many times on rivers when I've seen a small pike take the bait, I've tried to get it to let go; but they virtually have to be pulled out of the water before they do. If a pike drops a bait it is because it's

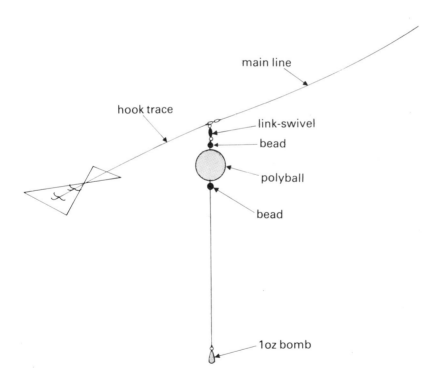

Fig. 12   Sunk paternoster rig.

not really hungry, rather than because it has met with a little resistance.

For all my deadbaiting I use the standard snap tackle with the bait always facing tail first up the trace. This makes for better casting and helps avoid deep hooking. With soft skinned baits, such as sardines, herrings and some coarse baits, it is best to tie them onto the trace (see Fig. 13) to make sure the bait does not come free during the cast, or when the pike picks up the bait.

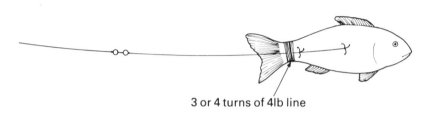

3 or 4 turns of 4lb line

Fig. 13 Soft bait set-up.

When using tough skinned baits such as mackerel and eel, the problem is to get the hooks out of the bait and into the pike's jaw. This can either be done by using a hair rig, or by using PVA (see Fig. 14). When using the PVA set-up, the hooks should be just nicked into the bait. The force of the cast is taken by two loops and PVA; when the bait hits the water the PVA melts, causing the loops to part, leaving the hooks only attached to the bait.

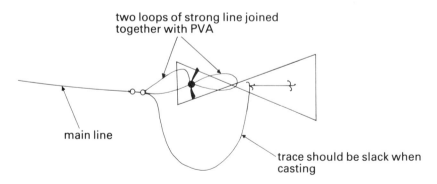

two loops of strong line joined together with PVA

main line

trace should be slack when casting

Fig. 14 PVA mackerel.

102

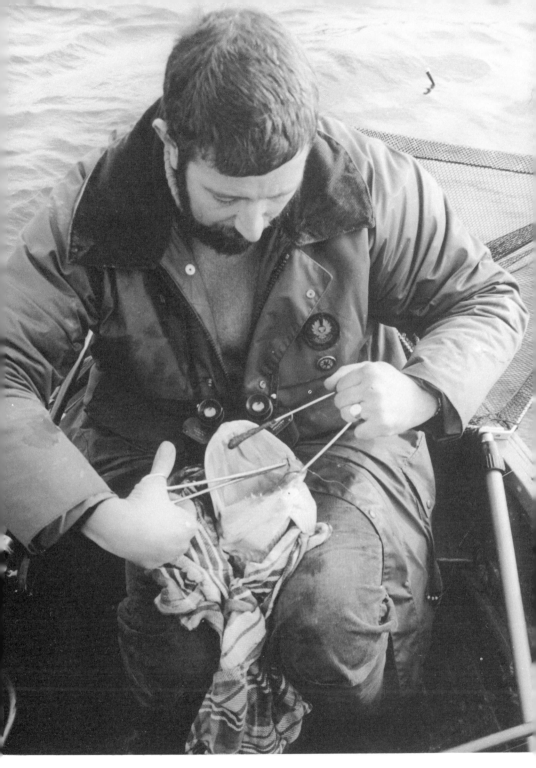

John Wilson extracting hooks from a pike. Note the padded end of the pike gag.

The two rivers I concentrate on are very different in character, and because of this my approach tends to differ. I like to be as flexible as possible; sometimes I use Avon tactics on the Stour, and vice versa. The Hampshire Avon is a much faster river than the Dorset Stour, and there tend to be far fewer pike swims. The approach I adopt is similar to my stillwater approach, in that I don't move around too much. I choose a pitch that I am confident holds pike and sit tight until those pike come to the feed. The Dorset Stour, on the other hand, is a much slower river with many pike-holding areas, and my approach is to fish many swims and find feeding pike, rather than wait for fish in one swim to come on the feed.

I think at this time it would be appropriate if I discussed what I believe to be the difference between the feeding habits of the river and stillwater pike. A pike's feeding habits demonstrate three **definite states:**

1) Non-feeding. In this state the chances of getting the pike to take a bait are extremely slim. On several occasions I have had a bait within inches of 20lb plus fish, and they either move slowly past the bait to a different lie, or simply ignore the bait completely. This happened to me recently on the Stour; I spotted a known fish of about 28lb lying in 2ft of water right under the bank. Keeping out of sight, and as quiet as possible, I lobbed a freelined smelt some 10yd upstream of the fish and watched with anticipation as the bait slowly rolled downstream towards the fish. The bait eventually settled some 6in from the pike's snout, which is where it stayed for half an hour until the pike swam slowly past it and out of sight.

2) Semi-feeding. In this state the pike can be tempted to feed if the right bait is presented correctly.

3) Feeding. In this state the pike should be fairly easy to tempt, as long as no stupid mistakes are made.

On stillwaters large pike spend a great deal of time in the non-feeding state, only a little time in the semi-feeding state, usually prior to the feeding state which will last as long as it takes for the pike to satisfy its hunger. On rivers, if water conditions are favourable, the pike spend far more time in the semi-feeding state than their stillwater brethren.

A 26½lb estate lake pike caught on deadbait free-lined in 11ft of water.

Pike in running water have to feed more because they use energy to combat the speed of the current. They spend more time in the semi-feeding state, as they tend to be more opportunistic feeders. To know this is of great importance as feeding and location are obviously linked. If a river pike is in the feeding state it will put up with the inconvenience of having to combat flowing water. If it is in the semi-feeding state it will move into slack, or slackish water, where it is comfortable to lie and have a chance of a meal. If it is in the non-feeding state the pike will move into the most comfortable swim available.

To locate pike in the feeding state one has to understand the movements of food fish. On the Stour the diet of large pike is mostly roach, bream and roach/bream hybrids. These species inhabit the medium-paced swims most of the time. During periods of high water they will move into the slack areas, and when the river is

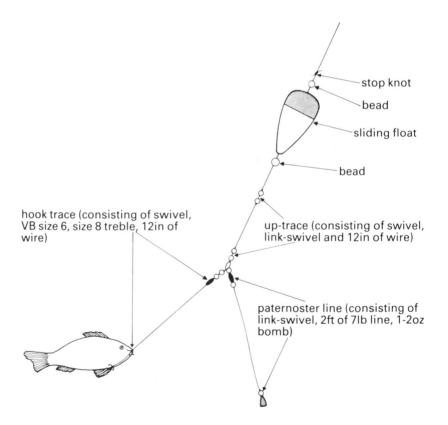

Fig. 15 Roving river paternoster.

very low they move out into the faster flow and the feeding pike will move with them.

Locating dace is a waste of time when in search of big pike. The dace are too small and too fast for a large pike to bother with. Small pike will be present but I have little interest in catching them.

The Avon is different from the Stour in as much as there are very few food fish between 8oz and 1lb 8oz. The small pike are all right for there are plenty of dace available to them, but the large fish have the choice of chub and bream in the 1lb 8oz – 4lb class. The chub are widespread throughout the whole river, so to find pike feeding on them would be extremely difficult. The bream, on the other hand, tend to shoal up in slackish or slow water. This is fortunate, for it means feeding pike will be present, and also semi-feeding pike because of the comfort of the swim.

To locate semi-feeding pike one does not have to necessarily fish in amongst the food fish. I've been told by two very good roach anglers that it is virtually impossible even to get a bite from roach or bream in my most reliable Stour pike swim. To find semi-feeding pike swims features to look out for include slackish water, medium-paced water adjacent to fast water, undercut banks, the ends of reed maces, in fact anywhere that reeds and overhanging trees are present. Don't worry too much about depth; most river pike that I catch come out of water no more than 4ft deep.

To tackle river pike I use four basic set-ups:

1) Paternoster livebait.
2) Wobbled deadbait.
3) Trotted livebait.
4) Float-wobbled bait.

The roving river paternoster (see Fig. 15) as it stands at the moment was developed by myself to combat the problems I encountered. At first glance it looks horribly complicated, with far too much iron-mongery, but it's very easy to set up and has not let me down once in three years. The stop knot, bead and sliding float are perfectly standard. The up-trace is essential to avoid bite-offs as you quite often actually see the pike take the livebait just under the surface in such shallow water. If you don't use an up-trace the pike will often take the main line as well as the bait, and the end result is a bite-off and a pike which has trebles in its mouth — something to be avoided at all costs.

The hook trace, which is simply clipped onto the up-trace, consists of a size 8 treble and a size 6 VB double. When fishing moving water, the bait has to be fished with the hook nearest the swivel in the mouth. If a treble is used then often more than one prong of the treble gets caught in the bait's mouth, thus making it impossible to pull the hooks out of the bait and into the pike's jaw.

The paternoster link is attached to the up-trace via a link swivel, which is easier than tying it direct, and also causes less tangles. The beauty of the set-up is that when moving swims the bait does not have to be removed from the hook; instead, the hook trace is unclipped from the up-trace and the bait with hooks still attached is put into the livebait bucket. The paternoster is undoubtedly the most reliable method when tackling a river, and if I was limited to using only one method it would be this one. Every swim is different and the paternoster is used in many different ways. Sometimes it pays to keep it static and other times it's best to keep it moving slowly, either by pulling it slowly back towards you or by using just enough lead to hold bottom and stret-pegging down the swim. If possible don't cast directly to where you think the pike should be; it is far better to cast several yards beyond and slowly pull the bait back to the favoured position.

For my wobbled deadbait fishing the end tackle is simplicity itself (see Fig. 16). The hook trace consists of size 8 treble, size 6 VB wire and the swivel tied directly to the main line. When the pike

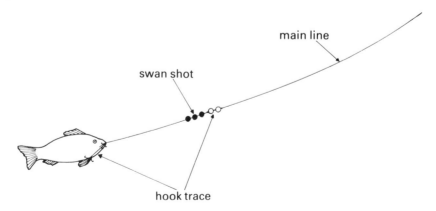

Fig. 16 Wobbled deadbait.

John Wilson shows how easy it is to pick up a medium-weight pike.

are really on the feed this can be a killing method and will out-fish all other methods. I prefer to use a medium-sized bait of about 4oz (anything smaller is difficult to work correctly, and anything bigger tends to make too much of a splash as it hits the water).

When you fish the wobbled deadbait try and give the bait as much life as possible, also try different types of retrieve. I like to keep my retrieve slow and exploring all depths. I do this by letting the bait fall to near the river bed, and then with a couple of jerks of the rod tip the bait is brought fluttering to the surface. It is then allowed to fall to the river bed again and the process is repeated over and over until the cast is fished out.

The next cast is made slightly downstream of the first, and so on, until the whole area is covered. Never be too eager to take the bait out of the water at the end of each cast, because often the take will come only feet from the bank. What also happens is that a pike will follow the bait to the bank but will not take it; if this does happen put the wobbling rod down and lower a paternoster livebait to where the pike was last seen, and the take should not be long in coming. The last time this happened to me the result was an incredibly fat fish of about 24lb 13oz.

One method I have not mentioned is static deadbaiting. It does catch fish, but in my opinion does not compare with paternoster livebait or a moving deadbait when fishing the rivers I fish.

The trotted livebait is not a method I use a great deal, but in some circumstances it's useful. It is best used as an early-season method when the bait can be worked between weed-beds effectively. Keep the bait fairly small, up to about 3oz, and make sure the float is cigar-shaped, as it will not then become snagged so easily if a hooked pike rushes through a weed-bed. (See Fig. 17.)

As a late-season method I use it when I think there could be a fish in shallow water close in to my own bank. I can then position myself some way upstream and trot the bait down to the fish, rather than risk spooking the pike by getting too close. I don't use the method when fishing the far bank simply because it's too expensive on livebaits.

The float-wobbled deadbait method was as usual discovered by accident. I noticed that when I trotted deadbaits an alarming amount of takes happened when the bait had just started to be retrieved; the bait would rise to the surface and bang! – the pike would hit it. The float-wobbled deadbait was a natural progression.

The best swims to use the method on are ones with a fair current.

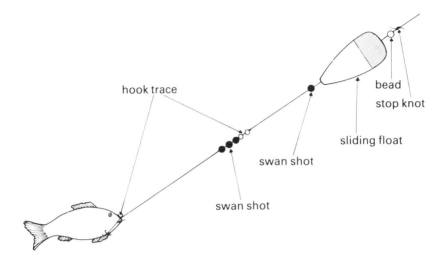

Fig. 17 Trotted livebait/float wobbled deadbait.

The bait is allowed to trot down for a couple of yards then held back hard and pulled back a little towards you. It's then allowed to travel downstream again and the process is repeated right down the swim. It's a very exciting method to use because the takes are normally near to the surface and are therefore indicated by a large swirl where the bait used to be, or, even better, the pike leaping clear of the water with the bait clamped between its jaws.

During the course of a day's roving I will probably use all the methods mentioned. If I'm adopting my static approach, most of the time I use two paternoster livebaits and try one of the other methods occasionally if things are a bit slow and I feel I'll benefit by ringing the changes.

The February–March period is when I expect to be most successful. This is not because the fish will be full of spawn and at their heaviest, but because I will have been fishing for a solid four months and by now I should have a pretty good picture of what is happening in the area. I should know what stretches of rivers are on form and also what has been caught from the stillwater.

The weather at this time of year is very unpredictable. Some years it is getting warmer and almost spring-like, and in other years, we experience sub-zero temperatures. This of course has an effect on the habits of the pike. If it is very cold it is normally dry, so the rivers will be in good condition, and although they won't be in great form there is always a chance of a big fish. The stillwaters, on the other hand could well be frozen; if not, sport is usually pretty unproductive. The gravel pit might produce a fish or two but the lake is a definite no-no in extremely cold weather.

If the weather is warm the stillwaters should be worth a try and the rivers, if not in flood, should be in form as well. Location on rivers might change but if the weather has been generally warm for most of the year the pike might be starting to move towards the spawning grounds. These are normally shallow slack areas with reeds present; some really good bags of fish can be taken when this occurs.

One very important factor which I've yet to mention is the size of bait. As I mentioned earlier, on the rivers the main part of a pike's diet consists of roach, bream, hybrids and chub. It makes sense to use bait of similar size to what the pike is used to eating. On many occasions I've introduced a small livebait into a swim and had no response, so I've substituted the small bait for a 6–8oz roach or bream and a take has been almost instant. I'm sure this is because a semi-feeding pike has been located and the pike does not really think it's worth its while to expend the energy chasing such a small meal; but if a decent meal is put in front of it, it will become worthwhile.

TACKLE

As far as tackle is concerned the pike angler has never had it so good. There are literally dozens of first-class rods and reels on the market, and thanks to E.T. there are lots of smaller items that can now be bought rather than made.

For 90 per cent of pike fishing a 12ft 2¼lb test-curve carbon rod will be the perfect tool. For some situations, such as extreme-range casting, drifting or when extra large baits are used, it might be useful to go up to a 3lb test-curve, but for my fishing the trusty 2¼ 12-footers do the job admirably.

Like rods, there are many reels on the market which are suitable for pike fishing. I've always used Mitchell 300s, and at present see no reason to change. They are strong, reliable and the deep spools have good line capacity. I've tried most of the well-known lines on the market and in my opinion the best all-round line is Sylcast. Compared to other lines its diameter is not particularly fine, but it is unbelievably strong and stays that way for a long time. This is especially important when deadbait wobbling, because the continual casting will ruin softer lines in a matter of days.

I use a 15lb test for most of my fishing; I know some of you will think this a little unsporting, but as I said earlier it is an unforgiveable crime to leave hooks in a pike's mouth, and by using the strength of line I use break-offs are virtually non- existent.

The only time I go lighter is when an extra long cast is essential;

Nick Putnam with a 28lb 15oz pike caught on hair mackerel from a Dorset club water.

then I use 11lb Sylcast. The hooks I use are Partridge semi-barbless trebles and Partridge VB doubles. These hooks may not be the sharpest on the market but because most of my fishing is at close range I feel that this does not cost me fish.

They are, however, very strong, and in three years I have not had one break. I tried some chemically-sharpened Japanese hooks last year, and the first fish I hooked was lost because the hook broke. After changing back to my Partridge semi-barbless, the next fish I had was a 29lb plus. If I hadn't hooked and lost the smaller fish I would have probably lost the big one; the thought does not please me.

I've tried most brands of wire on the market, some are very fine and a joy to use, but unfortunately if they become kinked they are incredibly weak. They don't kink very often but there is always the chance of a lively bait doing this, and if it does the end result is a dead pike with a mouth full of hooks.

I always check the trace before each cast, but despite this these ultra-fine wires have broken on me four times. The wire I've now settled upon is 30lb Berkley steel strand; in two years it has not let me down once. Swivels are either Berkley or Drennan diamond eyes; both are small and have never let me down.

For bite indication on stillwaters I now use the E.T. Backbiter for all my deadbaiting and sunk-paternoster work. On the rivers the float is always visible, if I want back-up indication I use an ordinary drop-off indicator. This has to be used in conjunction with a run clip because only one rod rest is used.

When fishing stillwaters I tend to use an enormous, fibre-glass matchman-type fishing box to keep my accessories in. It may not be very 'ultra-cult', but it keeps my stuff nice and dry. Inside the box I always keep a smaller rucksack which I use on the rivers.

When adopting a roving approach it is important to keep your tackle as light as possible. In the rucksack the only things I carry are a Stewart tackle box containing spare hooks, swivels, floats, wire etc, a weigh sling, a keep sack, set of Avon scales, scissors, forceps and deadbaits. If a large fish is caught then it is sacked for a short time while I go and fetch the camera from the car.

The only other tackle taken with me is a pair of tackled-up rods, landing net, two rod rests and the livebait bucket. With this amount of tackle, several miles of river can be covered without too much discomfort, and the only part of you which does suffer is the arm which carries the livebaits.

A 29lb 1oz Avon pike, caught by Mike Booth.

THE FUTURE OF PIKE FISHING
In the next few years I see pike fishing changing a great deal. For some people this will be a good thing, and for other pike anglers the change will not be so good. More trout fisheries will open their doors to the pike angler during the trout close season and I'm convinced future British records will come from these fisheries.

Commercial coarse fisheries will be specially stocked with outsize pike to tempt anglers from all over the country to part with their cash and visit the waters. This, at first, seems to be a good thing, but unfortunately lies will be reported to the press to attract more anglers to make money for the fisheries and fishery managers. A good example of this is a water not too far from where I live, which will remain nameless.

Concerning the waters I fish the future does not look good. The pike in the Hampshire Avon are under constant threat from salmon anglers and fishery managers, who seem to enjoy nothing more than murdering quality pike. The Dorset Stour is under constant threat of pollution; I've been told by a friend who works at a sewage works that it's only a matter of time. The Water Authority are also doing their best to ruin the river with mindless dredging and trying to alter the course of the river.

On the plus side, less pike are being killed by thoughtless anglers than ever before. This is mainly due to the efforts of the P.A.C. who have worked tirelessly to enlighten anglers about conservation.

The pike angler must also try to be as responsible as possible, especially when using livebaits. Livebaiting is not everyone's cup of tea, so don't aggravate the situation by using particularly outsize baits or too many normal-size baits. I always make sure the lid is kept on my livebait bucket so if another angler walks past he doesn't get the chance to get upset about what bait I'm using.

Pike and pike fishing will survive; as the years go by my enthusiasm and love for the species grows. I hope it is allowed to continue to do so for many years to come.

8
ROACH
by John Wilson

Had I been writing this chapter during the mid-1970s instead of the mid-1980s, there would have been a vast difference in specimen roach potential at most locations around the country, and just one decade has elapsed.

In those heydays, my local Norfolk rivers, the Wensum and Waveney, held unusually large numbers of wonderful roach, mostly all between 1 and 2½lb. It was, of course, a freak situation which never before and never again will be seen in those rivers. The massive old roach, survivors of the disease which ravaged the species all over southern England during the 1960s, slowly died off, leaving very little in their place. In fact chub have now invaded most of my favourite old roach swims, where I used to sit, and on a good day, with the river nicely coloured, actually *expect* to catch 2-pounders.

Even worse for these rivers, the upper Wensum and Waveney in particular (although similar symptoms are now common in the decline of many southern rivers), is that shoals of roach fry which should be seen each autumn for the roach size pyramid to continue are simply not nowadays in evidence. Where isolated concentrations of fry or young roach do occur, by the following year they have nearly all vanished. It is the opinion of some local anglers including myself that farming chemicals are responsible for this decline in river roach. Certainly there is a common factor, in that it seems to happen more severely in rivers which run through arable land. The run off from pesticides and insecticides has finally built up such chemical differences in the rivers, only adding to the nitrate problem, that, where once there was clean gravel, there is now a layer of dark blanketweed or algae beneath which little food exists.

It is rather ironic considering the upper Wensum was without question the most wonderful roach river in Britain throughout the 1970s. Now it must rate amongst the worst, save for a few whoppers which remain and which paradoxically actually offer the chance of a 3lb roach because they have few other roach to compete with for food. Yet to catch a dozen 6oz roach anywhere along its 30 miles above Norwich is next to impossible.

THE IMPORTANCE OF LOCATION

Now I have made a point of documenting this ten-year decline in one of my local rivers at the start of this chapter on river roach for one very good reason. It illustrates perfectly the need for first being aware of current highs and lows in a river's roach potential. Of course, it also illustrates the importance of actual location. It matters not how sweetly you can put a stick float through a lovely-looking roach glide, if there are no roach in the swim. Believe me, to catch big roach you really should start by thinking as simply as this. So learn from my misfortune and be prepared to put in the time required to first locate your quarry. You can try following up current stories of roach captures in your area which appear in the angling press, or do your own research by exploring all water courses which hint potential.

Even quite small streams can breed the occasional whoppers if the food source is abundant and angling pressure is minimal. I have caught several roach in excess of 2lb from swims so narrow between reedbeds that I could almost have jumped across. So never write off the streams. Compared to rivers where roach cannot be visually located, they are much more interesting and often more productive. Obviously, the more roach inhabiting a stretch, the less is the likelihood of a percentage growing on to specimen proportions, unless the water is exceptionally rich. So look more towards small concentrations of roach where individuals may grow large.

Close-season observations are always so worthwhile, particularly during the late spring when roach spawn and adult fish can actually be visually located on the shallows propagating their species. This really is the time for spotting big roach if your river does in fact breed them. During any settled period of warm weather during the

A good catch of fine quality roach.

latter part of May it will be worth taking a look at the spawning grounds, which, as far as rivers are concerned, will usually be along the shallowest, fastest reach, especially where willows and alders line the banks exposing their pinky-red fibrous roots beneath the surface. These provide a perfect matting for roach to deposit their eggs upon, and where roach stocks are heavy the crashings and shudderings of spawning fish is an unbelievably noisy affair. Dare I suggest that you even begin to feel like a peeping tom?

Once the fry have hatched, their growth rate varies considerably in different areas according to the food source available. Starting with algae and phytoplankton, it is followed by all the common fly larvae, particularly the midge, planktonic crustacea such as daphnia, molluscs, assellus, freshwater shrimp, and brine shrimps (as found in parts of the Norfolk Broads and other tidal waterways). Ultimate length for a well-proportioned roach is around 16–18in, although in most environments somewhere between 12 and 14in is the norm. Incidentally, it is a fact that a 12in roach, which should weigh well over the pound, is the heaviest of our freshwater species up to that length. After a couple more inches though, it is quickly overtaken by the sheer physical bulk of a carp.

HYBRIDS

If certain other species happen to be on the spawning beds at the same time as roach, then they will hybridize. The two most common hybrids are roach/rudd and roach/bream. Roach/chub are not unknown but very rare, because like the dace chub usually spawn much earlier than roach in lower water temperatures and so do not become mixed.

To distinguish between a true roach and rudd, look at the dorsal fin of the roach which when folded should not overlap the start of the anal fin. Generally, the fins of the roach are a much darker (crimson) red than those of the rudd which are all 'orangey' red. In different fisheries colouration can vary considerably, however, so it's best to compare first the physical differences. As the lips of roach are about level when the mouth is open, compared to the much-protruding bottom jaw of the rudd, there is usually little trouble in differentiating between the two. Roach/rudd hybrids, however, which tend to be a bland mixture of the general colour and shape of both, can sometimes be confusing. The fact that roach have level lips and a bream a protruding vacuum-type mouth is always the noticeable difference between these two species. The roach also has much larger scales, is much thicker in cross-section, and, apart from being generally more colourful, is not covered in thick protective slime like the bream. The hybrids are not so easily distinguished because they contain distinct features of both species. Some may appear more like off-colour but true roach, while others will be 'breamy'-looking. The best way to treat any fish which you first thought to be a roach but which on second glance seems a little strange, is to give it the benefit of the doubt and settle for a hybrid.

Although there is none at present, record fish status with separate categories for hybrids would undoubtedly add more spice to any freshwater scene. Without national recognition a roach/rudd hybrid is prized nowhere near as highly as a true model of either species, which is a great pity. Roach/rudd hybrids attain weights well in excess of 3lb and are delightful both to catch and admire.

Roach/bream hybrids fight like tigers, adding the dogged agility of the roach to the slabsided weight of the bream. They grow too, with specimens to over 7lb having been reported. Fish of 3–4lb are quite common in some waters.

THE CHALLENGE OF THE BIG ROACH
To most anglers there comes a time when the sight of a whopping great roach holds an endless fascination. Perhaps the fact that most of the fish which first fell to our crude approach as children were immature, silvery little roach has a lot to do with it. For, although young roach usually prove easy to catch, the challenge of hooking into a big one and see it come sliding over the waiting net is probably the ultimate goal of most freshwater anglers.

I know of many experienced anglers with huge pike, bream, tench, carp and even catfish to their credit who have yet to fulfil their ambition of landing a roach in excess of that magical 2lb barrier. It is like the 4-minute mile, or to hole in one at golf. The mere thought of what a whopper will look like laying there beaten in the landing net, shimmering silver and blue, is what turns small children into roach anglers for life.

In complete contrast to attaining a certain target with some other species, success with big roach does not make you want to move onto another. After a lifetime of learning the techniques to catch roach from a diversity of waters both small and large, fast and slow, you are so well equipped to tangle anywhere with the species that you find that in addition to the fish itself it is the finesse of technique and tackle control which has you well and truly hooked. To trot a bait downstream close to the bottom in fast water on a crisp winter's day, and to 'feel' the current pull line from a centre pin reel is a sport almost unto itself, and a circumstance in which I personally feel truly at peace with the world. When the float suddenly disappears half-way along the swim, and you strike to feel the power of a river roach in winter trim, there is no finer experience in freshwater fishing; although, to be fair, presenting the static led-

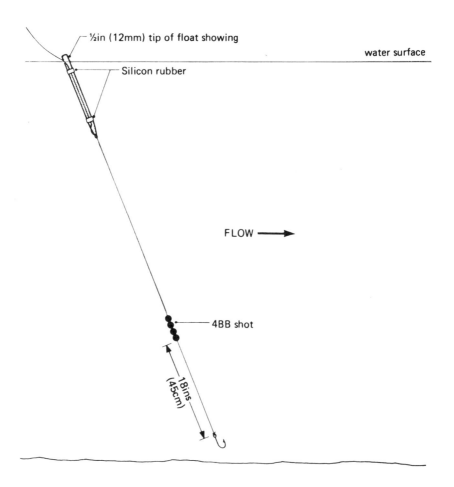

Fig. 18 *Summer fishing for roach.*

gered bait, a large lump of breadflake for preference, and using a delicate quiver tip for bite registration, produces the bigger fish more consistently (but more of this later).

LIGHT VALUES

Next to presenting the bait in a natural manner, both water and weather conditions play an important part; but actual light values are possibly the most important factor of all.

Being a shoal member and dependent on others for general awareness, anything which affects one generally affects all the others within seconds. So, if one fish is frightened by a 'silhouette on the skyline' of the angler who either sits too close to the water's edge or stands up when he should be crouching down, panic will quickly spread throughout the shoal and bites may stop.

Remember that smaller species like roach during their early years live on constant guard against predators such as eels, trout, chub, perch and pike, and water birds like herons and cormorants, to say nothing of being hooked by anglers. Of course, the reality of being grabbed by a pike lasts until the day even a big roach dies. So, as it gets older, it naturally becomes a very wary creature indeed. As it has already been through every kind of experience on the way to growing large, it will have seen its original shoal greatly depleted from perhaps as many as a thousand fingerlings to just a few dozen mature specimens. In small stillwaters, and particularly in streams, these numbers will of course be greatly reduced, and a shoal which starts out in hundreds can be reduced to just half a dozen large fish in as many years. Such a small shoal living in a rich environment would contain fish of a high average size. In fisheries with a poor food source an identical small group of roach might average out at no more than 12–14oz apiece.

Regardless of weight, however, fish which live in a minority are incredibly shy and suspicious of anything which threatens their existence. They need to be caught off guard, and there is no better time than in periods of low light values with a poor visibility beneath the surface, either at dawn or particularly dusk which is the favourite of all times for a wily old roach to oblige. During patches of heavy mists or fog, immediately after heavy flooding whilst the river or stream has that distinct 'smokey' look, are also good times. Fishing on into darkness sometimes offers even better prospects,

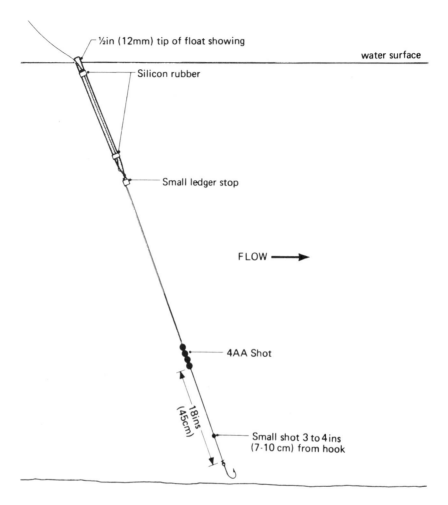

Fig. 19 Winter fishing for roach.

particularly when the river runs low and clear making a daytime assault out of the question.

Big roach will sometimes oblige when a really good chop sweeps down the river and ruffles the surface despite clear water conditions, and, of course, they are most vulnerable of all when they can be seen 'priming' or 'topping' on the surface. Unlike bream, which are renowned for failing to get their heads down and bite whilst rolling, with roach cavorting in the swim a bite is never far away. The fact that roach love to roll on the surface at dawn and dusk, whether they are 'nymphing' or simply jumping for the joy of

Nick Putnam with a lower Avon roach, weighing 2lb 10oz and taken on double maggot.

living, is very often the key to putting a whopper on the bank. In mere minutes from starting to fish, a big one can so quickly come your way, and of course knowing that the fish are actually in the swim and on the move for food gives enormous confidence. So always be on the look-out for rolling roach. Move to them immediately, should the swim you are fishing not produce bites. Always mentally log the whereabouts of rolling roach for use at a later date. 'Find 'em during the summer, and then catch 'em through the winter', is about the best motto I can offer in general terms.

So, then, having I hope itemised a few of the pertinent 'dos and don'ts, wheres and whens', what about the nitty gritty of 'how'? Well, as such, there is of course no best method, nor best rig. On the day, long trotting might well sort out the biggies if there is a good-sized shoal in the swim, and the river is nicely coloured with the weather mild. On another occasion, only ledgering with a bait completely static will be accepted. As a general rule, 'moving' baits in mild weather and 'static' in cold conditions would be a good rule of thumb. It works for me anyway.

Overall, however, I think a static bait will invariably turn up a much larger stamp of roach, particularly where small shoals are concerned, which may quickly become agitated by trotting, with its continual casting and retrieving. For me, a static bait means a thumbnail-sized piece of breadflake from a new loaf, as opposed to worms or maggots. I do use other baits for big roach and have taken quite a few on stewed wheat, for instance, but to pick just one there is nothing to touch flake which takes you right through the pain barrier of small unwanted fish to the biggies. So don't be afraid of using a large hook. Size 8 and 10s are the ones I use most.

BITE INTERPRETATION
Rather than skimp over several basic methods of presentation and do none of them justice, I am going to delve rather deeply into just one, and one which at the end of the day could mean several super roach in the net or simply dozens of missed bites. In fact more bites are missed or not even struck because anglers fail to interpret bite registration correctly, whilst quiver tip ledgering, than with any other method. So, because the angling press is continually showing diagrams of popular float rigs and how to shot a stick float or how to put a waggler through etc, I shall put all my eggs into the static bait

A specimen roach.

basket and suggest that during the winter months ledgering with breadflake on a swan shot paternoster fixed lead rig, and interpreting the ensuing bite via a built-in quiver tip, is, next to electro fishing, your best bet.

Free baiting is done with bread only, using old scraps well soaked and then squeezed between both hands till all the water is expelled. It is then mashed between the fingers – thus creating thousands of attractive particles all of which will sink immediately and not overfeed. Two or three balls of mash the size of a chicken egg go in at the start of a session, followed perhaps by more should numerous bites develop from what is obviously a large shoal of roach. In most circumstances, however, and where small shoals of a dozen or so roach are concerned, it pays to be miserly with free feed rather than to overfeed them.

Once a shoal or two have been located, a dose of free bait just before dark for several evenings running before actually fishing will usually bring immediate success. I like to keep several swims going in this way by free feeding at least a couple of days each week, so I can alternate and not put undue pressure on any particular swim.

For presentation, consider my simple paternoster ledger rig in Fig. 20, using one, two, three or four swan shot (depending on flow) and incorporating a tiny size 12 swivel as the junction between reel line, hook link and lead link. As can be seen from positions 1, 2 and 3 running ledgers are simply not functional in running water, because water pressure against the line plus the weight of lead required to 'just' hold bottom in the desired position are what is important. The line can never 'run' through a sliding link (except perhaps in position 1) because water pressure on the line would dislodge the swan shots long beforehand. So a fixed lead or paternoster is advisable from the start. Then you need not worry about such trivia as weed gathering around the ledger bead or swivel which should slide but cannot. It all makes not the slightest little bit of difference to a biting roach, which, giving any sort of positive bite at all, instantly dislodges the swan shots. Hence, it is important

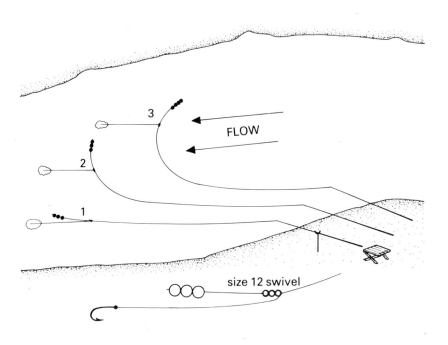

Fig. 20 Fixed lead/paternoster rig.

to have sufficient on the link to only 'just' hold bottom, and no more!

Now, the 'type' of bite experienced depends on how far out across the flow the ledger is positioned. In position 1, for instance, with both lead and bait lying immediately downstream, more or less in a direct line to the quiver tip, few slack line bites will occur. I suppose the odd suicidal roach might swim several feet dragging the swan shots with it against the flow, but I would not hang around waiting for too many of these. No, most bites in position 1 will register as 'positive' forward movements of the tip as a fish turns downstream or across current with the bait.

In position 2 with just a slight but appreciable bow in the line between top and lead, we can start to understand what happens.

A good condition 1lb 4oz roach.

The swan shots are now lying not directly above the bait but a little to one side as the flow bows the line inwards towards the bank. The tackle is now very sensitive and bites from roach moving off downstream, upstream or across current with the bait will immediately register on the quiver tip.

A sudden 'springback' and 'shaking' of the top after the lead has settled properly (and these bites sometimes occur within seconds of the lead catching bottom) means that a roach has sucked in the bait and made off quickly across the current. Really positive bites are shown by more gentle backward movements of the tip and are often immediately followed by the tip bending right round as a roach confidently turns downstream. You should not miss many of these.

The most difficult bites both to interpret and to convert into hooked roach come when the tackle is settled in position 3, a fair way out across the flow with the line pushed into an enormous 'bow' by the current.

This bow is, of course, exaggerated when the rod tip is positioned low to the water, submerging nearly all the line. So when fishing across the current try to angle the rod tip upwards, keeping as much line out of the water as possible. Many anglers, I think, have trouble believing the line does in fact follow this extreme curvature; but there is no other way of holding the lead well out in a strong flow than by letting out more line to alleviate current pressure. The line could not possibly, for instance, hold along angle A in Fig. 21 with so much water pressure against it, and unless a bow is allowed to alleviate that pressure (as in angle B) it will immediately be pushed downstream to angle C. Taking this into account and going back to Fig. 20, you can guess what happens when a roach moves off downstream with the bait as in position 3. There is firstly a slight forward (nodding) top movement as the bow is tightened, followed immediately by the quiver tip 'clanging' back as the leads become dislodged and swing round in the current. Roach which receive little angling pressure may still have the bait in their mouths and actually keep the tip pulling round once the leads have re-settled; but many will drop the bait within a second of the leads moving.

Roach which simply move across the current a little when the tackle is in position 3, as many do in a tight shoal because they cannot turn around, will only register that initial gentle 'ease back of the tip' as the bow tightens, and then promptly eject the bait upon feeling an increase in resistance before the leads are dislodged.

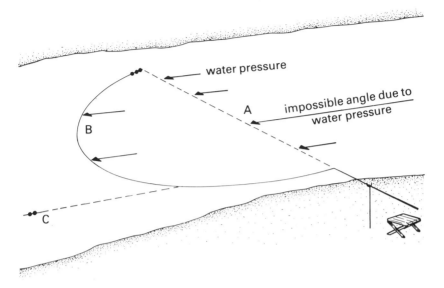

Fig. 21   Fishing across the current.

These are the bites you really need to convert into roach in the net, because on some days they are the only indications to strike 'at'.

Now, to really put the hook home and pick up the excess of line caused by water pressure calls for a hard, sweeping, backwards and upwards strike. To increase the 'striking arc' I prefer to position my quiver tip rod (a 12ft 1¼lb test-curve North Western Carbon with 20in of solid glass spliced in) at an angle of somewhere between 30 and 45° to the river, pointing downstream of course. On the strike I then lean forward slightly and really bang the rod back in a sweeping follow-through action. At times a break on the strike would seem inevitable, but so long as the tackle is sound there is nothing to worry about. Missing bite after bite, however, by half-hearted striking can prove most frustrating – particularly when many of the gentle, 'ease back' type of bites hardly seem worth hitting.

To illustrate these points about fishing across the current, let me recall a day's ledgering for chub and roach on the river Wensum at Costessey, with two friends. Bruce Vaughan and John Everard had travelled from Oxford to stay with me for the weekend, and I think it is fair to say that as both usually ledger very close into the bank in deep swims for roach in their local Thames, they were rather baffled by the bites from Wensum roach. Both were used to experiencing bites where the tip slowly or quickly, but positively, pulled round, just as in Fig. 20, position 1, like their deep, close-in local swims would have produced. But in much of the Wensum during the winter months the fish hang out in the middle of the river and not under the banks. So when both latched onto roach shoals during the late afternoon and subsequently missed bite after bite, to say they were perplexed is an understatement.

Poor old Bruce experimented a couple of dozen 'gentle dropbacks' on the quiver tip, but failed to strike at any because none materialised into a forward pull. When I told him afterwards that the bend contained a good shoal of roach to over 2½lb, he went mad. But that's roach fishing.

9
TENCH
by Bob Church

Have you noticed the ever-growing trend in coarse fishing? So many eager anglers are becoming specialists. It was 30 years ago as a keen young angler that I fell into this mould for the first time myself. I was an avid follower of the late great Dick Walker's every move in those days. It was the time that Dick was in his prime as a big-fish catcher, and specimen hunting was beginning to become known about through Dick's famous *Angling Times* column which ran for just over 30 years — what a feat that was.

I was a founder member of the now famous Northampton Specimen Group which was started in 1963. It remains a very strong club to this day, and just a couple of seasons back our member Alan Smith broke the national bream record, and Andy Barker had a 66½lb carp from Cassien. Being a member of a specimen group can help you a great deal to becoming a much better fish catcher. At each meeting members freely talk of their latest conquests and pass on information of tackle, methods, baits, waters and general hints, a great asset indeed.

In the last few years things have begun to change; many clubs are dropping the old 'specimen hunter' tag and instead are calling themselves specialist groups, clubs, or indeed just individual anglers.

Before I begin this chapter about tench, I have to say that tench fishing in the 1980s is far, far better in this country now than it has ever been. You could say the same about carp, but very few other species. Carp, of course, have been helped on by good stocking policies during the past 20 years, but why should tench grow much larger today without any such help?

Younger specialist tench fishers are perhaps not quite so aware that during the 1950s and 1960s it was a real milestone to crack the 6lb weight barrier. I believe that Dick Walker did achieve this. In those early days most of us had to be happy with building up a big score of 5lb plus specimens, and these were not too difficult to come by at a number of well-known waters. However, it was amazing how the weighing scales would stop at 5.12, 5.13, or 5.14.

We could theorise that tackle is so much better and that this helps in the downfall of larger, more wary, specimen tench. Like me, though, I am sure most of you will not go along with this argument, even though today's tackle is superb.

In the 50s and 60s many more roads, motorways and general buildings were constructed which created a need for far more raw materials than ever before; and so a great mass of gravel pits were dug out all around the country. Most certainly the rich aquatic food chain that exists at most gravel pits suits a very good growth rate for tench. I have seen this at first hand myself in that great chain of gravel pits in Gloucestershire, around the South Cerney area. Martin Pollard invited me to fish one of his gravel pits, and there were tench in there to near 11lb to be caught.

Martin, of course, runs both trout and coarse gravel pit fisheries and he is in a position to monitor growth rates better even than anglers. Regularly he would net his trout pits to remove unwanted coarse fish, and what did he find? Tench indeed. Such fine young fish, when moved to other waters, can of course go backwards in the growth/weight ratio.

So, as you can see, many of today's big tench in the 6–8lb bracket are coming from fairly new gravel pits which are no more than 20 to 30 years old. Information from *Angling Times* weekly catches highlights this.

What has been most baffling to me and many other older tench fishers is why we should be catching larger fish from the old, established stillwaters. I refer to places like Tring, Southill and my own local Sywell reservoir. I must admit that this really had me guessing. I then began to realise that tench live to a good age and it needed a completely new breeding stock to change things. This is what happened at Sywell; the new batch of young tench grew on very fast reaching the 5–8lb bracket in five to six years.

How do I approach the eve of the opening of a new season? By the beginning of June when out trout fly fishing I start to get such thoughts as 'roll on the 16th', so I can try once again for my beloved

This fast-growing gravel pit tench of 5lb 9oz came from one of the prolific South Cerney pits.

tench. As you may guess, my choice of water would be the well known Sywell reservoir, an 80-acre water close to my home.

My son Stephen is a typical example of the new type of specialist angler. After many years of not wanting to come fishing with me (well, hardly at all), during the last five years or so you would think he had invented the sport. But I must give him his due; he is getting pretty good. He began to walk his new spaniel round Sywell each evening to try to observe tench movement. With about a week to go before the 16th, he found a spot where many good tench were rolling each evening at dusk. He told me all about it and then asked if I wanted to fish the swim with him on opening day.

The next evening we went to the water together and the swim he pointed out was one I had never fished before. Tench were there in good numbers all right, rising and rolling just like trout in a stew pond. 'You have done well to find this spot, Steve,' I praised. 'Now you have found them we must make sure they stay here until opening morning.' The secret is to bait each evening with just enough groundbait to keep them interested in staying around.

I suggested a bold move of concocting our own recipe of attractor. Powdered concentrated caramel and prawn were two new ingredients for me to use in a tench groundbait. I mixed this with the very fine Tima bleak mix and finally my old tench favourite, dried blood. The blood, of course, gave the whole mixture a very dark colour, something my experience tells me is a must for tench. I have always found white or yellow groundbaits soon scare tench away.

For three evenings prior to the 16th, we baited up an hour before dusk, and the tench stayed. Now all we had to do in these times of high-pressure fishing was to make sure we got to the swim before anyone else. I took a gamble on the early morning of the 15th, leaving a large notice pegged in the spot which said, 'Baited Swim, Please Honour — Bob Church'. I still have faith in human nature, for when I arrived after tea-time on Friday the whole of Sywell was like a pegged-down match with brolly camps all around the lake, but our spot was still vacant. I had never seen so many anglers fishing at Sywell. See what I mean about the growth in numbers of specialists!

Steve had to go out to dinner and said he would arrive around midnight. There is a rule of the Wellingborough Nene Club, who own the fishery rights at the reservoir, that there shall be no fishing until 4am. By the sound of the continuous buzzing of electric bite alarms and the constant flashing of torches in the darkness I doubt if many kept to the rule. I was pleased that the hours of darkness were so short and at 4am Steve and I began fishing in our double swim, which took two rods apiece.

Thirteen tench for 70lb, a very high average weight and just a few hours' fishing at Sywell.

We used our own 11ft carbon or boron specimen rods, Mitchell 300 or 400 reels (they are still the best), 5lb breaking strain line, open end medium size swim feeders on nylon and tiny swivel links, and a plastic ledger stop 18in from a size 12 eyed specimen hook completed the tackle. I personally see no reason whatsoever to change from the ultra-sensitive dough bobbin bite indicator, which I used. Steve preferred his monkey climbers. Bait was to be either sweetcorn or maggots in white or yellow. The groundbait feeder filler was the exact same we had been putting in each night.

As I have come to expect from this bold-biting and hard-fighting fish they were quite eager to take our baits. We were casting about 35yd into 10ft of water, tightening down to the feeder, then giving the line a sharp 2ft pull; this releases the feeder contents and brings the hookbait right into the centre of the free offerings. Bites came regularly to maggot; we used two each yellow and white cocktails. The sweetcorn rod did not give a bite in the first 45 minutes so we changed all to maggot.

There is one drawback with fishing two rods when the fish are on; sooner or later a tench hits the second rod as you are unhooking a fish taken on the first. When the tench run very large on average, as they do at Sywell, breakages do occur, and this is not good, for a scared fish can move the shoal.

I did have an advantage over Steve because on my side of the swim I had a large bistort weed-bed to my left. Any fish coming out from this natural holding spot came to my bait first. By 10am I had taken 13 specimen tench for 70lb with weights going 6.5, 6.4, 6.2, 5.14, 5.11, 5.5, 5.5, 5.4, 5.3, 5.2, 5.1, 4.14 and a tiddler of 3.6. Steve had 6.1, 5.14, 5.9, and one of 4.14. As you can see, the average weight was very high, the highest I have known for the water. My 6.5 fish was a male; it put up an incredible fight and is one of the largest I know to have been caught anywhere.

Throughout the session my bites were confident, but not so Steve's. As I pointed out there is a certain amount of resistance when the monkey climber indicator slides up its rod. When he eventually changed to the dough bobbin he had better bites.

Another thing that proved itself is that using my giant keepnet I can retain a good catch for a few hours without any of them coming to any harm. My net is 12ft in length by 27in in diameter and the support rings are rigid always holding the net in an erect position (see Fig. 22). I staked the net out in 3ft of water along a rush bed where the fish were happy in their short stay.

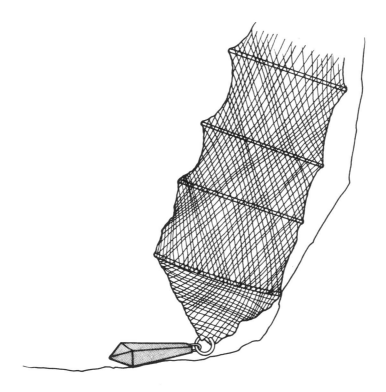

Fig. 22 A keepnet with torpedo lead attached.

I find the best procedure after netting a good fish is to have a weigh bag and Avon scales handy. Weigh the fish quickly before putting it in the keepnet and jot down the weight on a list. In this way if you want a quick photograph at the end of the session you don't need to subject the fish to any further stress.

It seems quite clear to me that the tench is No. 3 on the specialist angler's list, with carp and pike leading the way. The tench, though, does seem to have the fastest growth in interest.

INDEX

Arlesey Lake 80, 85
Artificial lures 88

Baits
  natural 10
  particle 8, 9 – 10, 52
  specials 10
Barbel 7 – 19
  baits 8 – 11
  distribution 7 – 8
  feeding patterns 9
  handling 19
  location 8
  playing 17
  tackle 11 – 17
  tactics 11 – 16
  winter fishing for 17 – 19
Block end feeders 10, *11*
Boileys 36, 52
Bolt rig 16, 36
Bread 24, 52, 126
Bream 20 – 35
  baits 23 – 26
  feeding routes 22
  float fishing 32 – 35
  location 22 – 23
  tackle 26 – 35
  technique 26 – 35
Broadlands Lake 29

Bullhead 52
Buzzers 36

Carp 36 − 47
  bait 37 − 38
  feeding times 38 − 40
  location 36 − 38
  technique 37 − 38
Casters 9, 23, 24, 34, 87
Cheese 52, 53, 75
Chick peas 38
Chopped ham with pork 10
Chub 48 − 66
  bait 50 − 54
  diet 50
  feeding habits 50
  fly fishing for 58
  location 54 − 57
  spawning 49
  tackle 62
  technique 58
Crayfish 10, 52, 53, 57

Danish blue cheese paste 10
Deadbait 76, 85, 96, 100, 107
Dorset Stour 7, 19, 95, 107, 116
Driftbeater float *34*

Eel 67 − 78
  baits 75 − 76
  feeding habits 74
  location 70, 72 − 75
  tackle 70 − 72
  technique 77 − 78
  time of day to fish 76 − 77
Elvers 52

Feeder rig *14*
Field beans 42
Fixed lead/paternoster rig *128*
Fixed paternoster 27, *28*
Float-wobbled bait 107, 110 − 111
Free baiting 127

Glow-bobbin 30
Great Ouse, Upper 54
Groundbaiting 10, 35, 60, 62, 68, 136
Grubs 52

Hair rig 16, 36, 102
Hampshire Avon 7, 19, 95, 107, 116
Hemp 9, 38, 52
High nutritive value baits 10, 24, 52
Hollow-tip float *35*
Hucklesbrook lake 80, 87

Isotopes 13

Keepnet 138, *139*
Kennet 7

Lamprey larvae 10
Landing net *62*
Ledger rig *13*, 14, 77
Ledgering 26 – 32, 58, 126, 127, 131
Livebait 85, 96, 100, 107
Loaches 52
Lobworms 10, 24, 69, 76, 80, 85
Long trotting 59 – 64, 126
Luncheon meat 9, 53
Lures 88 – 89

Maggots 9, 10, 23, 24, 38, 52, 68, 73, 86
Minnows 10, 52, 68
Mixed pigeon feed 42

Pastes 52
Paternoster livebait 107, 111
Paternoster rig 101, 108, 127, 128˙
Perch 79 – 94
   bait 84 – 90
   location 81 – 82, 84, 90
   when to fish 82 – 84, 90
Pet biscuits 43 – 44
Pike 95 – 116
   bait 96, 100 – 101, 112
   diet 106 – 107
   feeding habits 104 – 107

gag *103*
location 96, 107
tackle 101 – 104, 107 – 110, 112 – 114
Prebaiting 23, 24, 52
PVA 10, 102

Quiver tips 13, 123, 132

Roach 117 – 132
    hybrids 120 – 121
    light values and 123 – 126
    location 118 – 120
    spawning 118 – 120
    tackle *122*, *124*, 126
    technique 126 – 132
Roving river paternoster *106*, 107
Royal Fishery 11
Rudd 120

Severn 7, 11
Slugs 10, 52, 57
Spinning 88
Static deadbaiting 110
Sunk paternoster rig *101*
Sweetcorn 9, 52
Swimfeeder rig 26, *27*
Sywell reservoir 134 – 139

Tares 9, 52
Tench 133 – 139
    location 134
    tackle 138
Thames 7, 8
Trent 7
Trotted livebait 107, 110
Trotting rig *13*

Waveney 117
Weights 14
Wensum 117
Wobbled deadbait 107, 108 – 110
Worms 9, 24, 52, 75, 76, 85